Zaha Hadid

Zaha Hadid

The Complete Buildings and Projects

Essay by Aaron Betsky

With 428 illustrations, 328 in colour

Thames and Hudson

© 1998 Thames and Hudson Ltd, London
Texts and images © 1998 Zaha Hadid
Introduction © 1998 Aaron Betsky

British Library Cataloguing-in-Publication Data
A catalogue record for this book is available from the British Library.

ISBN 0-500-28084-3

Book design by Adam Hay, London
Printed and bound in Italy

CONTENTS

Introduction
BEYOND 89 DEGREES
Aaron Betsky

The film, on the one hand, extends our comprehension of the necessities which rule our lives; on the other hand, it manages to assure us of an immense and unexpected field of action. Our taverns and our metropolitan streets, our offices and furnished rooms, our railroad stations and our factories appeared to have us locked up hopelessly. Then came the film and burst this prison-world asunder by the dynamite of the tenth of a second, so that now, in the midst of its far-flung ruins and debris, we calmly and adventurously go travelling. With the close-up, space expands; with slow motion, movement is extended. The enlargement of a snapshot does not simply render more precise what in any case was visible, though unclear: it reveals entirely new structural formations of the subject. So, too, slow motion not only presents familiar qualities of movement but reveals in them entirely unknown ones 'which, far from looking like retarded rapid movements, give the effect of singularly gliding, floating, supernatural motions'. Evidently a different nature opens itself to the camera than opens to the naked eye – if only because an unconsciously penetrated space is substituted for a space consciously explored by men.[1]

The Explosion of a Tenth of a Second

Zaha Hadid is a great cinematographer. She sees like a camera. She perceives the city in slow motion, in pans, swoops and close-ups, in jump-cuts and narrative rhythms. As she draws the world around her, she draws out its unconscious spaces. She finds what is latent in the constructions of our modern world and storyboards them into utopias. She boldly explores, she slows down and accelerates the rhythms of everyday life, and she subjects her environment to the surgical exposition of architecture as a form of representation. She builds the explosion of a tenth of a second.

This does not mean that she is not an architect. Zaha Hadid aims to build, and her images are part of the process that moves towards construction. She does not, however, propose inserting an autonomous object into a blank site. Instead, her buildings are intensifications that lead to extensions. She compresses all the energies that cause the building to appear, from its programme to its technological infrastructure. Her buildings are free to reach out from this density to create spaces that are free of encumbrances. Where there was once (the potential for) private activity, walls and pipes, there are now shards and planes that slice through the landscape to open up a space we did not know could exist.

Hadid has constructed her career in architecture in a similar manner. She has folded the memories of a youth spent on woven carpets into a training at London's Architectural Association. She has used the forms of early twentieth-century artists as the building blocks out of which she has erected her palaces of abstracted memories. She has drawn the energies of the city and the heavy contours of the landscape around her like a cloak, and then used that force as the starting point for explorations into an unknown territory towards which her angular forms point.

One might say that Zaha Hadid is a modernist, designing lofts tied to technological cores as a celebration of the new.[2] Hadid has no truck with typologies, applied orders, implied assumptions or gravity: she believes that we could and should build a better world, one marked by freedom, above all else. We would be liberated from the past, from the constraints of social convention, from physical laws, and free of our bodies. Architecture, for modernists such as Hadid, is the always fragmentary construction of such a world.

The Three Modes of Modernism

Traditionally, there are three aspects to such modernism. First, its adherents believe in new structures. By harnessing technology, a good modernist posits, we can use our resources (including ourselves) more efficiently to create the maximum amount of surplus, whether of space or of value. This 'too much' is that which is the heroic reality of the always new, the future, the utopian. It is that which has no shape and comes about by reducing form to its minimum. Second, the modernist believes in new ways of seeing. Perhaps the world is already new, but we just don't recognize it as such. We see only what we have been trained to perceive. If only we can look in fresh ways, we can change the world by just that act. We need to open our eyes, our ears and our minds to the realities of our existence. Then we will already be free. Third, the modernist wishes to represent the reality of modernity. Fusing the first two aspects, she or he transforms our new perceptions into representations for the forms we have created. Such shapes are the prototypes for a reality in which things have become rearranged and dissolved to the point that all but the new disappears. By representing new things in new ways, we can build a new world and inhabit it, if only with our eyes.

It is this third aspect that characterizes Zaha Hadid. She does not invent

new forms of construction or technology; she shows us a world in new ways by representing it in a radical manner. She finds the roots of modernism in the dissolution of both subject and object and draws them out onto the stage of the modern landscape, which she reshapes as a place in which we can boldly go wandering.

The models for such modernism go back at least to the Baroque, when subject and object first lost their unquestioned authority. Instead of the human body, which stood before God in a world of sin, there was only the continuity of the real into which the self became folded:

> Matter thus offers an infinitely porous, spongy, or cavernous texture without emptiness, caverns endlessly contained in other caverns: no matter how small, each body contains a world pierced with irregular passages, surrounded and penetrated by an increasingly vapourous fluid, the totality of the universe resembling a 'pond of matter in which there exists different flows and waves' (Leibniz).[3]

Architecture attempts to make this flow of energy present, to catch it in its myriad forms:

> The Baroque invents the infinite work or process. The problem is not how to finish a fold, but how to continue it, to have it go through the ceiling, how to bring it to infinity . . . [the fold] determines and materializes Form. It produces a form of expression, a Gestaltung, the genetic element or infinite line of inflection, the curve with a unique variable.[4]

The industrial revolution of course built such a world of chaos, removing meaning or value from each object or individual and folding it into the flow of capital. As a result, architecture increasingly dissolved into fields of glass, steel and concrete, flowing around the last vestiges of form and burying them behind the accumulations of consumer goods. It is these flows that Zaha Hadid builds.

Bringing the Outside(r) in

Yet Hadid's work does not have only the Western roots associated with modernity. Born in Iraq, she speaks of her fascination with the Persian carpets of her youth, the intricate patterns that defeated comprehension and embodied the collaborative efforts of hands transforming reality into a sensuous surface, simple spaces into lush ones. Note, coincidently, that was also women's work.[5]

In the narrative unfolding of Hadid's work, one can also draw a comparison to Chinese and Japanese scroll paintings. Modernism proposes that we construct sense out of the accretion of everyday activities that continually change our reality, rather than fixing a particular order onto things. This is a method of working that the painters of scrolls knew well. They slithered in and out of their works, focusing on small details, showing scenes several times from different angles, stringing together landscapes out of isolated elements. The sweeps of echoing lines folded into a vision that altered and returned a world, transformed, back to the viewer.

The Peak – Night (1982–83)

All of these traditions were available to the artists of the early twentieth century, and their art provides clues to Hadid's pictorial building blocks. Whether in Cubism, Expressionism or Suprematism, abstract fragments were assembled into a narrative structure. These artists blew up their world – Duchamp's *Nude Descending a Staircase* is Hadid's grandmother.

Hadid's most immediate parentage is that of the Architectural Association in London. She studied there during a period when the school was at its peak as the world's centre of architectural experimentation. Building on the legacy of Archigram, students and teachers such as Peter Cook, Rem Koolhaas, Bernard Tschumi and Nigel Coates transcribed the convulsions of the modern world into the subject and the form of their work. Daring to be modernist all over again, they sought to capture the energy of all our changing activities by telling stories about them, and in so doing added a narrative viewpoint to the attempt to give shape to modernity. Whether the works were anecdotal and convoluted (Tschumi), a mythical collage (Koolhaas) or a manifesto (Cook), they all incorporated multiple perspectives, sweeping and expressive forms, and technological frameworks into images whose representation described rather than defined.

Condensed Collages

It is in this context that Zaha Hadid's work took shape. Her first notable project, her thesis design for a bridge over the Thames (Malevich's Tektonik, 1976–77; p. 16) is undoubtedly indebted to her association with Rem Koolhaas – she collaborated with the Office of Metropolitan Architecture for three years – in the way in which it foregrounds a geometry reduced to its essence, literally evoking the Suprematist work of Malevich. Her painting of the bridge looks like the Malevich airplanes that could also be sculptures or homes. The neutrality of the image is intentional, as she saw the building as a 'social condenser', to use a phrase then popular at the Architectural Association. The building itself is a modernist loft that folds back on itself to bring different programme elements (which she does not actually show) into close contact with each other. What astounds us as viewers, however, are not the project's functional aspirations or its quotations of the past, but the image itself: it holds the page and eye with a resolute statement of the new.

In several projects after her graduation, Hadid continued to develop her narrative stance more fully into a spatial language. The forms of 59 Eaton Place (1981–82; p. 19), an apartment design for her brother, directly evoke an IRA bomb that had exploded on the site. The drawing itself is an explosion, and the elements it places on the page are fragments from this most modern release of energy. In what was to become a central theme in Hadid's architecture, the objects condense and the city's forms turn into furniture. These interior pieces then move back out to take their place as Pop Art elements, a stage set for the re-occupation of a modern city.

Hadid developed the 59 Eaton Place drawings further into her vision of Halkin Place (1985; p. 28). In a rooftop view, the viewer soars above the eaves of the city's rowhouses to have a Peter-Pan view of a city coming apart at the seams, a perspective that lets Hadid's fragments of a modernist utopia re-inhabit their historical forms.

Hadid's proposal for the new residence for the Irish Prime Minister (1979–80; p. 18) introduced collage into her work. Representational elements (tiles, globes, bricks) populate a simple cube through which a long curving wall cuts to open up the project's narrative. Instead of telling us about the programme or the site, Hadid evokes the cosmopolitan nature of the residence; rather than give us the plot, she sets the scene.

Her proposal for the Grand Buildings project in London's Trafalgar Square (1985; p. 25) summarizes many of her achievements and shows her ability to re-imagine the urban landscape. The painting is a diptych that depicts the building from at least five perspectives. It also shows the city peeling away from itself in both a right-side-up and a bottom-up view, creating the unsettling effect of not knowing what is the reflection and what is the preferred ground of the painting. By combining the cleverness of an Escher drawing with the aspirations of a Constructivist composition, Hadid delaminates the city.

Hadid has a programmatic rationale for this manner of representation: the Grand Buildings project was something that would put the activities and forms of Trafalgar Square into a dense composition that would free up layers of open spaces to allow the city to breathe into the building while its aggressive shapes moved out into the urban terrain. Opening up the city at the seams, where the reality we experience and the fantasy of a new projection or building meet, became a recurrent subject of her paintings. In this instance she accomplished this within the image itself, leaving Trafalgar Square to its over-touristed reality and her building in the utopian realm of unfulfilled fantasies.

The summation of these early works took two forms. The first was a painting that presented all of her projects to that point, The World (89 Degrees) (1983; p. 24). In it Hadid imagines our global reality as a collection of her designs as we might see them from a helicopter or a missile shooting off into space. As the world turns, its landscape heaves up into fragments of new geometries. The real world becomes Hadidland, where gravity disappears, perspective warps, lines converge, and there is no definition of scale or activity. This is not a specific scene of functions and forms, but a constellation of possible compositions that together form a veritable landscape: a space shaped by human hands into an artificial depiction of the physical environment in which we live.

The second summation made Hadid famous. Her winning entry for the Hong Kong Peak competition (1983; p. 20) proved to thousands of architects and design students (including this author) that the techniques she had been developing were a new form of architecture. Situated at the highest point of the colony, the project was itself a summation of the site as well as of all those programmes that jettisoned the mundane demands of existence in favour of a purely hedonistic collection of forms. The building was a facility that aimed to delight and discipline the body in a form that appeared socially acceptable.

Hadid's architecture embodied this programme and site in tubes that stacked up on top of each other like a pile of wooden beams on a construction site. They extended the verticality of the site in cantilevers and stratified spaces. The interstices of the forms articulated the Peak's function as a social club where activities intersected, while the beams' movement seemed to capture and solidify the trajectory of bodies in motion. It was a building that brought human and mountain together to test each other. It did not just 'crown the brow'; it pulled the very Peak apart so that we, like latter-day Titans, could do battle with it.

Hadid laid out this vision in a set of very large paintings that seemed to aspire to the scale of the Peak itself. Although the architect emphasized the rational nature of her construction, the drawings pulled the parts and pieces apart, exploding its site and its programme. In one painting Hadid showed elements of the club becoming part of downtown Hong Kong, while the metropolis's skyscrapers below became abstract planes that rotated, flew off and actually turned into the building blocks for the Peak. In these instances Hadid put forward an architecture that represented the artificial landscape of that or any metropolis as an assembly of abstract geometric forms. These shards of the new pointed towards a more open, intense and unstable arrangement of space.

Setting Sail on a Sea of Gestures

In the following decade Hadid expanded these themes in buildings, designs and proposals around the world, a number of which were in Germany. These included her two largest built projects to date, the IBA Housing Block in Berlin (1986; p. 38) and the Vitra Fire Station in Weil am Rhein (1990–94; p. 62). While the former built the basic forms used in the Grand Buildings design, the latter pointed the direction to a new phase of her work.

The projects for Berlin Victoria (1988; p. 49), Hamburg Haffenstrasse (1989; p. 52) and Düsseldorf (1989–93; p. 68) had in common what had by now become Hadid's signature prow shapes, loft-like spaces around eccentric cores, public spaces brought into the building and shapes extending out into the city. Over the years these forms took on an almost stylistic cast, yet they also changed character. They became lighter, more transparent and more layered. To some degree this was the result of larger and in most cases more conventional programmes. These office buildings and apartment blocks had few hybrid elements, so it was perhaps difficult to develop a narrative representation of them.

One also sensed a shift in focus. Where Hadid's earlier buildings were collages assembled out of disparate elements, her forms now seemed to evolve as singular gestures. To Hadid this was the result of seeing her work as a form of landscape, or shaping of the land. While the Berlin Victoria City Areal still followed the recipe of intensification and extrusion Hadid had first proposed in the Grand Buildings scheme, the large complexes in Düsseldorf and Frankfurt read like fragments of a modernist iceberg whose clefts leave the edges as openings. These fissures reveal the partial nature of each building. In the Düsseldorf project, the complex's various functions accrue similar forms, which are sheered off into bridges, walkways and public buildings that are unified in their free exploration of space. Whether in the public realm or in the office towers, everything is part of the same universe of forms.

Hadid's use of colour also began to change. After the hot image of the London ICA project (1988; p. 46) and the colour-coded fragments that still haunted both Berlin buildings, the other German designs were remarkably soft in their colourations. This was partially because glass now predominated, and perhaps also because of the relatively grey environment of German cities. It also, however, seemed to mark a cooling down of Hadid's palette: tones and tonalities, folds of continual forms and modulated volumes displaced collages of shards.

These developments culminated in the Vitra Fire Station. When one sees it from Frank Gehry's celebrated all-white museum, one is most aware of the prow-like shape of the building. In reality – and Hadid's drawings make this clear – the fire station has been conceptually sheered off from the factory blocks next to it and shot through with a curving walkway that leads back to the museum and around the complex. It is an eruption out of its place that freezes the muteness of the factory walls as tilting enclosures. The building opens up views along the fire station's contours, rather than standing against them. This geological formation continues on the inside, where the larger spaces for the fire trucks curve into the shower and lounge areas, and the stairs step up with the volumes towards the second floor.

Hadid proved with Vitra that she could build a landscape. Although the

Vitra Fire Station (1990–94)

Habitable Bridge (1996)

forms may appear familiar, they are a long way from the constructed assemblages of her early work. Instead of building on the land, opening up new spaces and inserting forms that reared up with aggressive challenges to their surroundings, she now drew her forms out from the site, moulded them out of functions and used spatial logic to create monumental built facts. Her architecture became reminiscent of how fields rise up over hills and caves open up below them, of how rivers move through undulating landscapes and peaks provide a sense of orientation. Perhaps Hadid realized that the 'explosion of a tenth of a second' revealed not so much the construction of the human psyche as it did the nature of the built environment as a sedimentation of human habitation that follows rules analogous to those in inorganic nature.[6] She found free spaces not in the fragments of a utopia, but in the exploration of what already exists.

Spiralling into Control

After Vitra, spirals begin to appear in Hadid's work, in the folded metal plate that enclosed the Blueprint Pavilion (1995; p. 108), the curling up of the

'urban jewels' in the Cardiff Bay Opera House (1994–96; p. 118) and the Victoria and Albert Museum Boilerhouse Addition's tight sequence of spaces (1996; p. 124). After wandering in the landscape, Hadid's buildings seem to want to make the landscape their own by wrapping it around the programmes and then using the surroundings to shelter or contain space. In the V & A project, the gallery spaces reach up beyond the rooftops in the same way they did in Halkin Place. In the Cardiff Bay Opera House spirals enclose the grand space of the main hall; in the Blueprint Pavilion, they created an aedicular presence for the fair stand.

Although most of her recent works are large buildings, Hadid draws them as transparent volumes. Instead of the weighty presence of tectonic plates, she now suggests that the manipulation of geometry and structure could liberate a space from its confines. The preoccupation with continuity of a landscape becomes recast as open reaches and interior volumes. Many of the drawings associated with these projects have white lines on black surfaces, as if they were but sketches of possibilities open to interpretation. The certainties of her early projects have given way to the gestural exploration of abstract openness.

11

This translucent, gemlike quality reached a culmination in Hadid's proposals for the Hackney Empire theatre complex (1997; p. 163) and the Cincinnati Contemporary Arts Centre (1998; p. 168). Here the skins dissolve into nothing more than the interface between the energy of the city and the interior. These forces become more and more localized in ramps and spiralling volumes. Folding and interlocking, positive forms (walls, floors and ceilings) and negative spaces (inhabitable spaces) turn into eels slithering around each other in ever more dense, and yet fully lucid, spatial organizations.

At the same time, the tubular forms of her earlier projects turn into dominant features. They are bundled together to form the Spittelau Viaducts in Vienna (1994; p. 96) and the Habitable Bridge project (1996; p. 135). Though to some extent the beams recall the slabs of the Peak project, they are now much denser and more tightly packed; circulation and usable space become virtually indistinguishable. They also emphasize the horizontal movement through space over the vertical build-up of form. In the 1997 project for a landscape exhibition in Germany (p. 151), they merged with Hadid's previous interests in the making of a landscape to create a great curved plane.

Towards a New Landscape

Landscape has become a dominant pre-occupation in Hadid's work. If the volumes of her designs are increasingly fluid, so are their exteriors. In projects like the Museum of Islamic Arts in Qatar (1997; p. 156), the building becomes no more or less than a ripple undulating out of the site, moving up to encompass spaces and then dying back down into the ground. Courtyard slots

weave space and solid together like a Persian carpet, but also like rivers or lakes, and move in and out of land. Like ripples in clothing or the forms of the Verner Panton chairs she adores, these buildings are moulds of the programme that rise up only as far as they must to accommodate use, but then reveal the beauty of the body inherent in the movement itself.

Inside this new world, however, there is a different reality. It is one Hadid has most fully explored in such recent projects as her scheme for an exhibit in the London Millennium Dome (to be completed in 2000). The complex interweaving of spaces and forms is smoothed over by the landscapelike skins, but with a flip of a wall, the contours of landscape become overhanging prows. Hadid has not forgotten her desire to gesture beyond the limitations of site and programme to create structures that seem larger and more open than we expect from a confined building.

Most of Hadid's recent projects thus appear to have replaced slabs, prows and blocks with spirals and tubes. Motion and gesture have replaced form as dominant elements, and the work is more open, tentative and lyrical. Opening up the urban landscape, unfolding the energies of the modern metropolis and creating a visionary world, Hadid explores the spatial possibilities of such an architecture in forms that have their own typology, structure and – dare one say it – stylistic properties.

The manner in which she presents this work parallels its intentions. Over the years Hadid has involved herself less and less with the execution of her paintings and drawings. She now prefers to work, like a Renaissance master, as the head of an atelier. She sketches and does 'all the precise lines' that

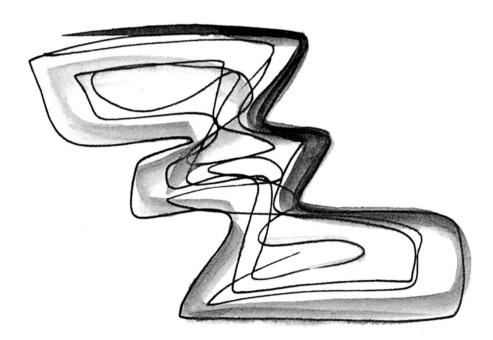

Boilerhouse Extension, Victoria and Albert Museum (1996)

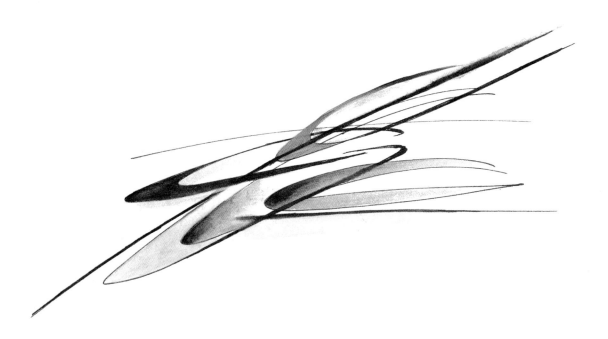

Museum of Islamic Arts, Doha, Qatar (1997)

indicate her design objectives;[7] her co-workers render the work at a larger scale and fill in the spaces between her gestures. There is less detail in the work, less differentiation and less colour. Having moved from multicoloured and heavily painted collages to monochrome washes, she now produces paintings that are only white lines on black paper, ghosts of a future city.

Screen Gems

Despite her continuing painterly approach, Hadid now also makes use of the computer to advance her aims. The latest software allows her to take the existing landscape and unfold it, to pan, swoop, swerve, cut, slow down and speed up. In many ways the computer fulfils Benjamin's promise, especially as the separation between perception, representation and realization dissolves. The computer is a way of registering facts about our environments; it makes visible forces that are otherwise too abstract to see; it allows us to form and reform those facts however we choose; it can then quantify these critical representations into buildable qualities. Thus the new comes out of a manipulation of the representation of what already exists.

What disappears in the process is the hand of the maker. This Benjamin also predicted, but it would seem particularly ironic in this case because of Hadid's heroic stance as a maker of outrageous structures. To a certain extent this is not something that she can avoid. The latest computer programs can render what Hadid had constructed with such care in the 1970s and 1980s

into a common mode of presentation. Everyone today sees their buildings from swooping helicopters, and many designers follow the stress points of metal and stone to create undulating, attenuated and prow-like structures. At the same time, Hadid is responsible for engendering a style that now forms office buildings, homes and fast-food franchises from Seattle to Singapore.

Instead of the framed image, the critical painting or the film, the model for her work is now the screen that collects the flows of data into moments of light and dark. The reflection of her own face is barely visible on that screen. Most of the space is dark, and the lines point not out of the cadaster of the space of representation, but in towards the flows of information. The question Zaha Hadid now faces is whether she can solidify these flows into form. Can she find the landscape beyond the physical metropolis? Can she form the spaces that open up not as modernist lofts, but as the fragments of tuned and wired environments suspended in global relationships? Can she make something real and free out of what is hard to grasp and constrained by the logic of technology and capital?

When Hadid summed up her and our world together in 1983, she had confidence in the power of her painting to re-assemble the disparate pieces of our reality into a new one. She is poised to realize many of her dreams, and her ability to do so owes a great deal to the tremendous freedom computers have given us not only to imagine new worlds but also to construct them. Even if we miss the visionary painter of the early 1980s, we must recognize that the visible evidence of her signature on paper or canvas has disappeared exactly because her vision can now take concrete shape. As paintings disappear into computer drawings, their imagined world begins to appear.

In her recent projects Hadid seems to be moving beyond landscape into a new kind of space. It is one that is at once dense and open, defined and indefinite, real and virtual. Its shape is still only a promise, one that will soon be realized. What world awaits beyond 89 degrees, beyond right angles and skewed geometries, and beyond the event horizon in which human activities solidify into form, remains for Zaha Hadid to see and then present to us in her luscious lines.

Notes

1 Walter Benjamin, 'Art in the Age of Mechanical Reproduction', in *Illuminations*,
   trans. Harry Zorn (New York: Schocken Books), pp. 217–51, p. 236.
2 The loft is the modernist space par excellence, as it is an industrial, open and functional
   space that frees us from the distinctions between programmes, private and public, and
   decoration. It is the building block not only of Hadid's work but also of such other late
   modernists as Coop Himmelb(l)au. I discuss the significance of the loft in greater detail
   in *Coop Himmelb(l)au* (London: Architectural Review Press, 1998).
3 Gilles Deleuze, *The Fold: Leibniz and the Baroque*, trans. Tom Conley
   (Minneapolis: University of Minnesota Press, 1993), p. 5.
4 *Ibid.*, pp. 34–35.
5 Conversation with the author, 14 December 1997.
6 See Manuel De Landa, 'Nonorganic Form', in *Zone 6: Incorporations*
   (New York: Zone Press, 1992), pp. 128–67.
7 Conversation with the author, 16 December 1997.

Models of Lycée Français Charles de Gaulle, Spittelau Viaducts, Pancras Lane [opposite]

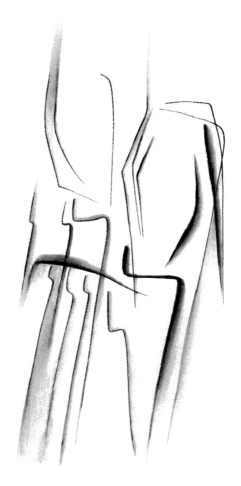

Philharmonic Hall, Luxembourg (1997)

The Complete Buildings and Projects

MALEVICH'S TEKTONIK

London, 1976–77

For my graduation project from the Architectural Association, I wanted to explore the 'mutation' factor for the programme requirements of a hotel on the Hungerford Bridge over the Thames. The horizontal 'tektonik' conforms to and makes use of the apparently random composition of Suprematist forms to meet the demands of the programme and the site.

The bridge links the nineteenth-century side of the river with the South Bank, which is dominated by the Brutalist forms of a 1950s arts complex. The structure's fourteen levels systematically adhere to the tektonik, turning all conceivable constraints into new possibilities for space.

The project has particular resonance with my later projects: first, in the *Great Utopia* show at the Guggenheim [p. 81], in which I was able to realize some of these tektoniks in concrete form, and second, in the Habitable Bridge project [p. 135], which considered the possibilities of a mixed-use development over the Thames.

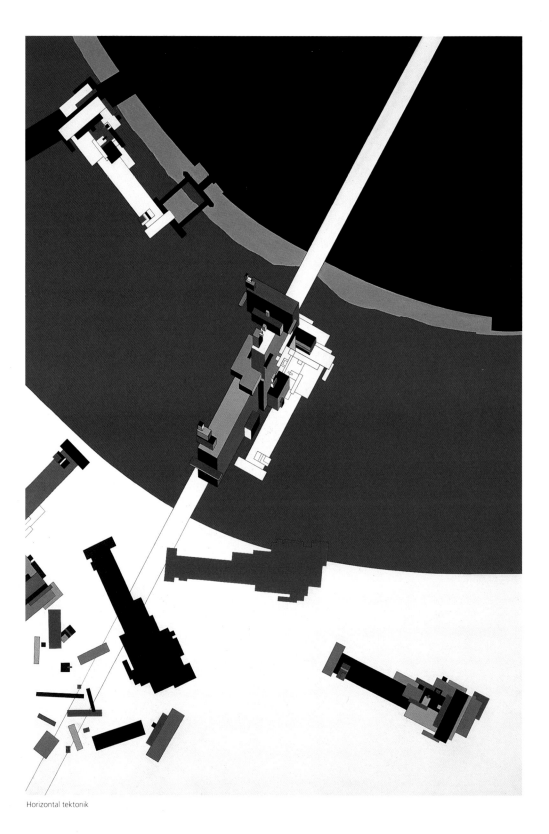

Horizontal tektonik

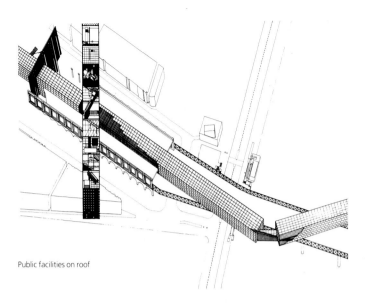

Public facilities on roof

MUSEUM OF THE NINETEENTH CENTURY

London, 1977–78

One of my first ideological and conjectural projects, in which I sought to establish principles for the role that architecture should play in cities at the end of the twentieth century. I was particularly interested in the problems of historical and cultural context. The archetype of the nineteenth-century museum was thus explored in two ways: through the elaboration of the precise social scenario of the metropolitan location, and through the display of a symbolic sensitivity, an aspect that appeared to be absent in the work of the contextualist architects at that time.

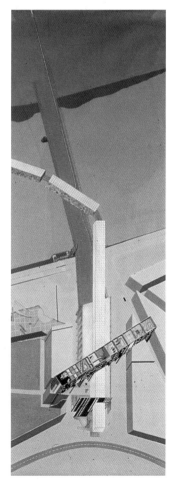

DUTCH PARLIAMENT EXTENSION

The Hague, 1978–79

The Office for Metropolitan Architecture (OMA):
Zaha Hadid, Rem Koolhaas, Elia Zenghelis

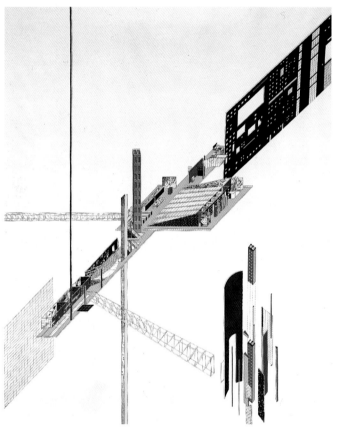

Situated within a rectangular 'fortress' in the centre of the Hague, the politically distinct branches of the Dutch parliament and government were housed in a single complex called the Binnenhof. To separate these two politically opposing branches, a triangular site was acquired to allow for an expansion of parliamentary accommodation. The programme therefore involved working within existing structures while making the parliament spatially autonomous. This was achieved by creating a gap in the Binnenhof that is occupied by two slabs: a horizontal element – a glass-brick podium that contains a variety of functions and that acts as a covered forum for political activity – and a small skyscraper of oval rooms. The two structures are unified by an assembly space that bridges the general public and government officials, and an ambulatory running through one slab allows circulation.

IRISH PRIME MINISTER'S RESIDENCE

Dublin (Phoenix Park), 1979–80

For my first major project, a new residence and state function room for the Irish Prime Minister, the objective was to create a weight-lessness, freedom from the stress of public life. Both buildings, though connected by a road and walkway, needed to retain their privacy. Placed within the existing walled garden, the new guest-house is screened from the prime minister's residence by the main reception rooms. The guest-house rooms are located around its perimeter, apart from the reception block and master suite, which 'float' over the garden.

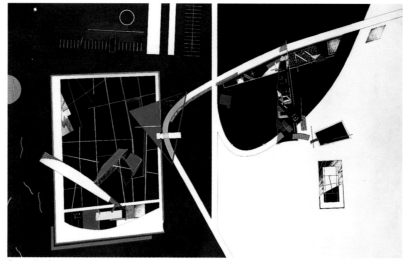

Composite plan

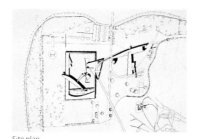

Site plan

Ground-floor plan

Aerial view

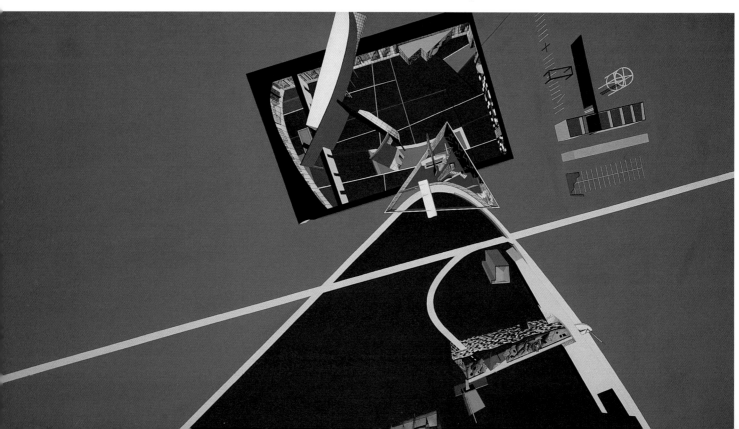

59 EATON PLACE

London, 1981–82

An explosion at the Italian Consulate at 38 Eaton Place provided the main inspiration for our renovation of an elegant turn-of-the-century town house on a sterile, white-washed street in Belgravia. The apartment is contained on three floors, which we inverted conceptually as three vertical zones. Our intervention in these spaces was intended to provide a certain newness, which we achieved by introducing materials such as silk and stone on the ground and top floors, as well as by inserting a new staircase in the lobby and dining-room area to open the public domain up into the middle level.

Park isometric

Plot of internal elements

PARC DE LA VILLETTE

Paris, 1982–83

For a competition to design the plan and elements of a park located outside central Paris's most visited area and devoted to science, we created floating pieces that would move across the site's flat terrain. The green plateaux in a field form a new type of garden, suspended rather than hanging. Together, these pieces function like calligraphy on the land, which is dictated by mechanical systems that are at once controlled (by humans) and random (by nature). Picnic areas, fast-food restaurants and information kiosks orbit within their own galaxy in contrast to a long monochrome 'planetary strip'. Appropriate to a project conceived for the future, there is a 'discovery garden', which condenses all the park's functions and landscapes.

THE PEAK

Hong Kong, 1982–83

Overall isometric

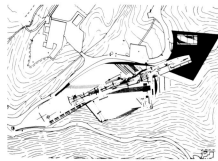
Site plan

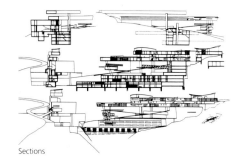
Sections

Slabs

A Suprematist geology – materials that are impacted vertically and horizontally – characterizes this cliff-top resort loftily located above the congested city. The architecture cuts through traditional principles and reconstitutes new ones, defies nature and resists destroying it.

Like the mountain, the building is stratified, with each layer defining a function: the first and second levels contain apartments, the third layer – a 13-metre-high void suspended between the second and the penthouse storeys – features the club. The void is a landscape within

which functions – exercise platforms, snack bar, library – are suspended like planets. The upper strata contain penthouse apartments.

Offering and symbolizing the pinnacle of the high life, the Peak's beams and voids are a gentle seismic shift on an immovable mass.

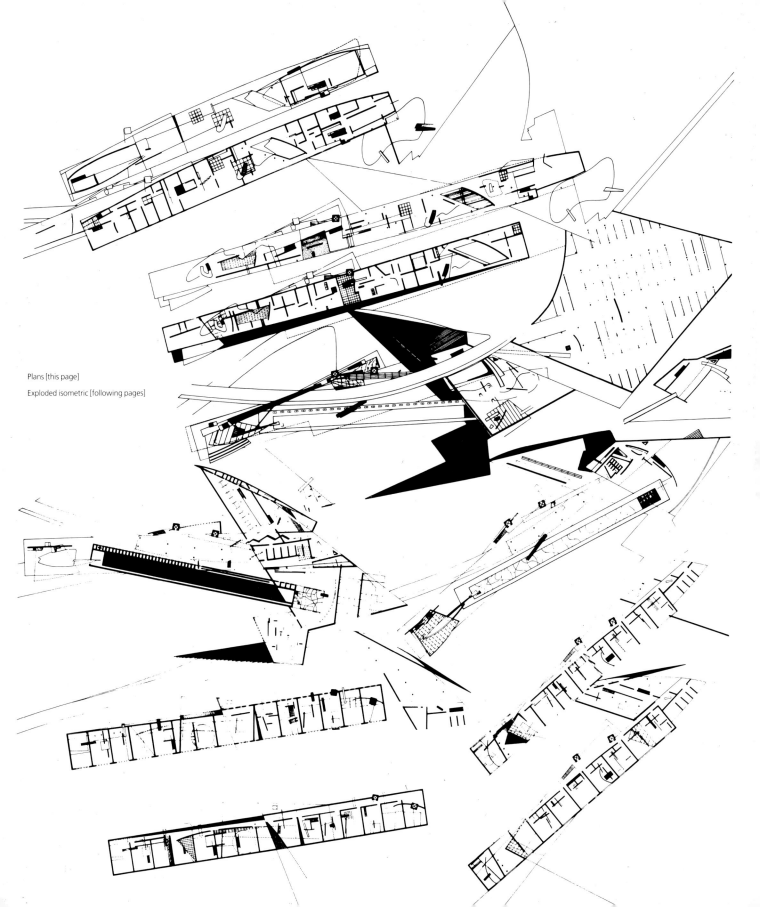

Plans [this page]

Exploded isometric [following pages]

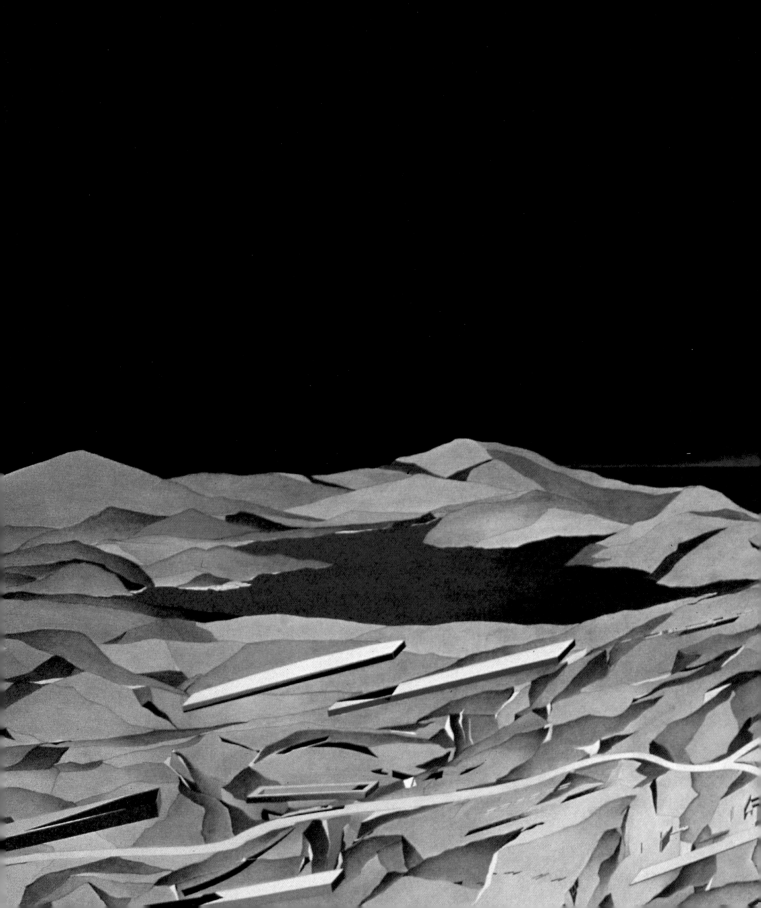

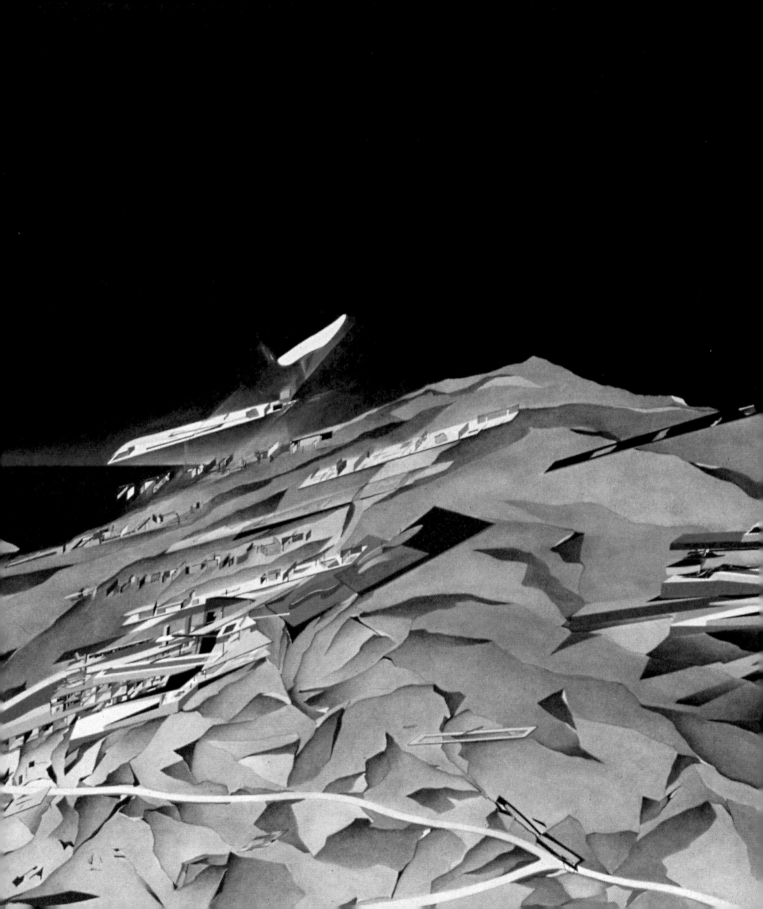

THE WORLD
(89 DEGREES)

1983

This painting represents the culmination of a seven-year exploration into architecture's uncharted territories that began with my work as a student at London's Architectural Association. Technology's rapid development and our ever-changing life styles created a fundamentally new and exhilarating backdrop for building, and in this new world context I felt we must re-investigate the aborted and untested experiments of modernism – not to resurrect them but to unveil new fields of building. The painting compresses and expands projects I had carried out over the last seven years.

GRAND BUILDINGS

Trafalgar Square, London, 1985

Schemes to recapture London's most famous square continue to this day. In the hope that outdated planning restraints might be abandoned, we presented a proposal that celebrated the dynamic possibilities of the urban landscape by extending the public realm into professional offices, thereby pushing forward the frontier where modern architecture can

Exploded isometric of public levels

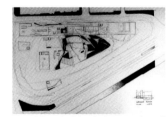

Ground-floor plan [above]   Skyline view [below]

contribute to the quality of city life. A public podium, slabs of offices and towers are the central characteristics of the buildings. Beneath the towers, which are topped by penthouses, are subterranean lobbies. A shopping concourse peels up, gently curving around the site's perimeter and enclosing a new public domain as it winds up to the roof, which features a public terrace that overlooks the mire of cars below. As one's vantage-point moves around the square, the towers appear to mutate from shards that penetrate the square's surface into a single solid mass.

25

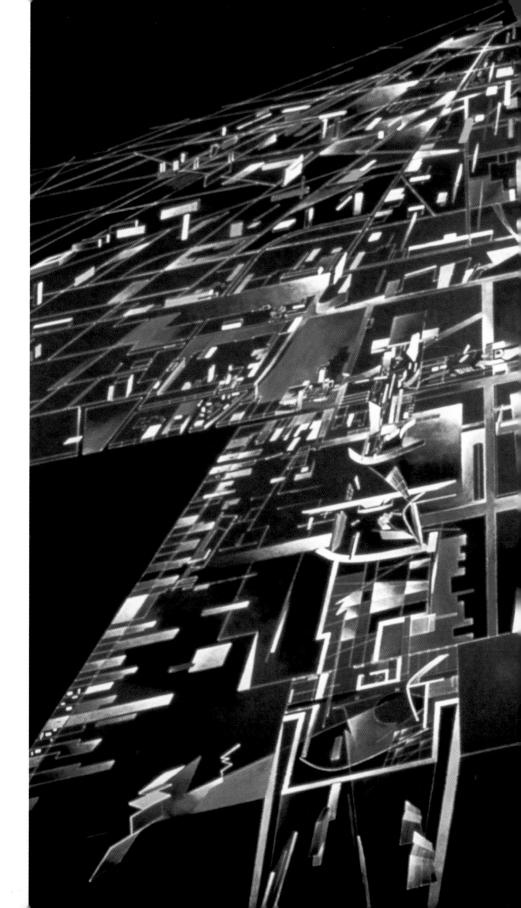

HALKIN PLACE

London, 1985

This study considers London at various levels, from small housing sites to larger urban schemes. We envisage a roofscape [right] that relates to the sky and its immediate urban condition – some roofs are habitable, others not. (This idea anticipates our concept for La Fenice [p. 140]). In a metropolis where land is scarce and planning restrictions are severe, these elevated sites are considered sites in themselves, with spaces divided vertically into indoor and outdoor zones. In the scenario of Halkin Place, the penthouse's spaces are sandwiched between the existing and the new roofs.

MELBURY COURT

London, 1985

This design aimed to explode the rigid box rooms of a small flat in a post-war, purpose-built flat. Two curved glass walls were stretched across the existing apartment, occasionally overlapping, to create a generously fluid space around the central light well. Furniture is on tracks or pivots to allow spatial and functional flexibility in the living areas.

Study model

TENTS AND CURTAINS

Milan Triennale, 1985

This exhibition gave us the opportunity to create a modern contrast to the Victorian notion of tents, which so often characterized the interiors of the period. Our scheme inserts a plastic structure within a pre-existing space. Intended to be viewed from above, the stucture's plan embraces the space by means of its exclusion – the opposite effect of the enclosure created by the Victorians' curtains and tents.

KYOTO INSTALLATIONS

Kyoto, 1985

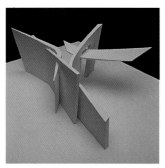

Study model

The installation is a fragment of the ideas that would reach fruition in the Cathcart Road project [p. 30], just as the Osaka Folly [p. 60] served as a test for design principles later employed at the Vitra Fire Station [p. 62]. Seeking new ways to articulate space within a confined context, we used curved walls to warp or bend space (like the Melbury Court project [opposite]) and canopies to mark the entrance.

View from exterior

Edra furniture

24 CATHCART ROAD

London, 1985–86

This International Style residence provided the backdrop for the first material display of my 'Suprematist geology', an extension of my exploration at 59 Eaton Place [p. 19]. The ensemble included *Bitar* furniture [p. 170], which did not act as sculptural objects in a neutral container; rather, the extra-large pieces created a dynamic space of their own. Pivoting, sliding and swivelling, a storage wall further animated the space with the actual physical movements of its doors and cabinets.

Sperm table

Overall interior plan

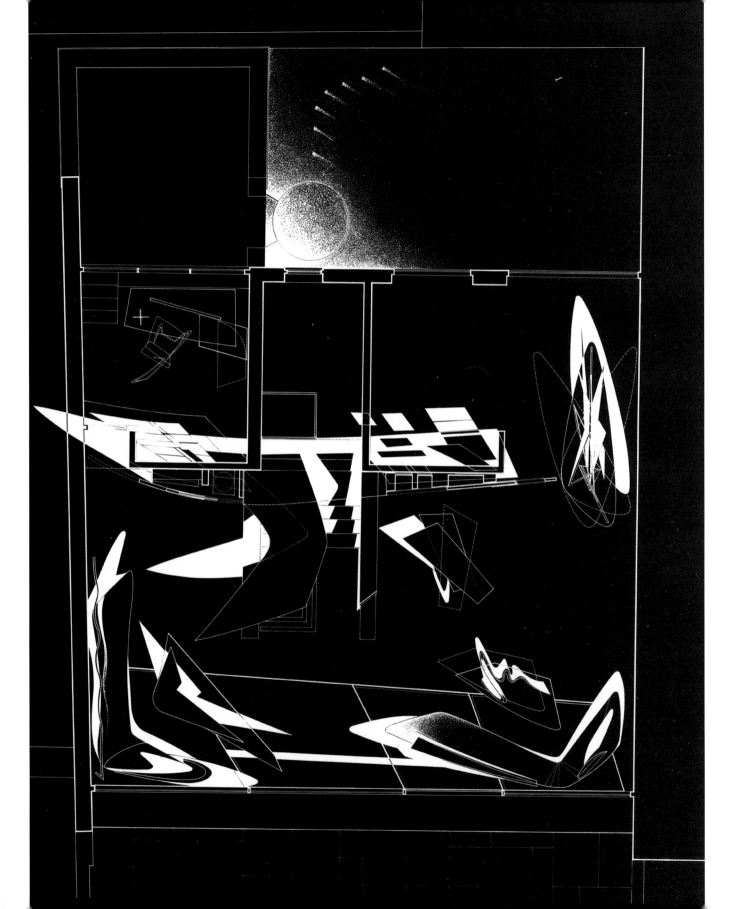

HAMBURG DOCKLANDS

Hamburg, 1986

During the late 1980s there was tremendous interest in revitalizing waterfront areas in numerous cities in Europe and America. As part of two workshops set up in Hamburg to explore the possible re-uses of these districts, we were asked to consider ways in which the city's historic old harbour area, particularly the former warehouse district of Speicherstadt, could be master planned to regenerate the area and accommodate a wide range of mixed uses.

The openness and large scale of the harbour front, as well as its integration into the city centre, raised a number of interesting problems that we addressed in various ways in the Haffenstrasse Development [p. 52] and in Cologne's Rheinhafen [p. 88]. By pushing the city's urban context into the harbour to capitalize on the spaces particular

to it – views, openness, ever-present water – we sought new geometries and zones for redevelopment that would create not only a new style of urban living but an entirely new dynamic within the city's fabric.

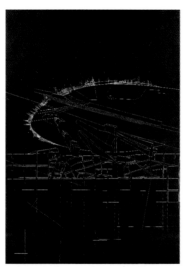

Preliminary study

Study of elevational rotation

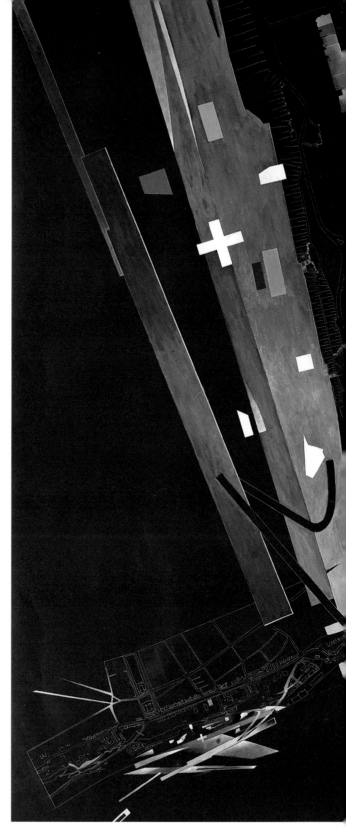

Site study

32

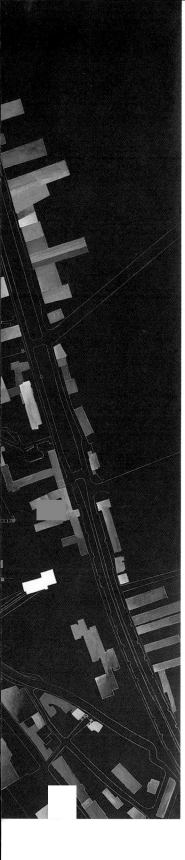

NEW YORK, MANHATTAN: A NEW CALLIGRAPHY OF PLAN

1986

Relating to a proposal for the reconstruction of a hotel, this sketch outlines possibilities and variations for redefining 'hotel' and 'metropolitan living' as a specific series of confined explosions. The point of departure was Corbusier's Ville Radieuse for Manhattan, which I believe fundamentally misjudges New York's urban conditions. Because Manhattan is a multilayered city, intensified by its urban density, built interventions should be considered to be like condensed explosions. Whereas Corbusier's vision was to dissolve the city, only to replace it with a carpet of bland modernism, I believe it is possible to sustain the intensity of the metropolis without eroding the grid that holds it together.

KURFÜRSTENDAMM 70

Berlin, 1986

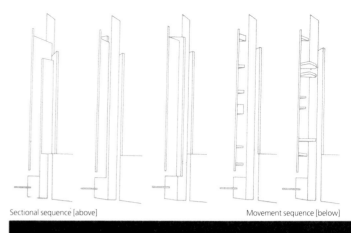

Sectional sequence [above]   Movement sequence [below]

Street view

Plan elements

The constraints of an extremely narrow site (2.7 × 16 metres) gave rise to our design of a compressed 'sandwich' structure that comprised a series of planes, spaces and uses. The horizontal planes of the sandwich are the basis for the floor plan, which establishes the separation of circulation and movement from the office spaces. Vertically, the sandwich of spaces differentiates between the ground-floor plan for the public entry and the cantilevered building above, which houses offices and a double-height office at the top. The lobby and entrance are raised above the ground and reached by a ramp, liberating the plan from the ground, a nod to the Russian Suprematists. The structure above is pulled away from a new back wall, and the gap above this ramp reveals the main entrance.

The plan is gently bowed and moves out towards the corner; thus the floor area reaches its maximum at the top and creates a dynamism that rejects the usual office-block repetition. The long street elevation has a transparent surface – a structural mesh of aluminium extrusions suspended from the top – that becomes an illuminated glass box through which the interior's activities can be detected.

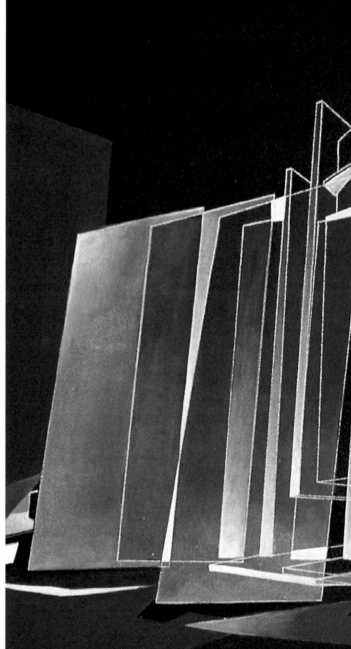

34

Studies

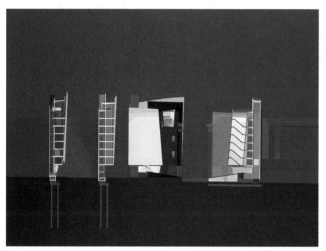

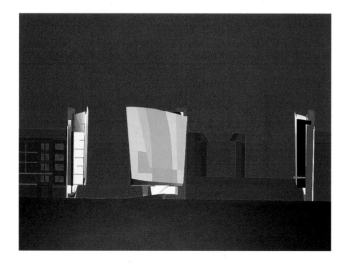

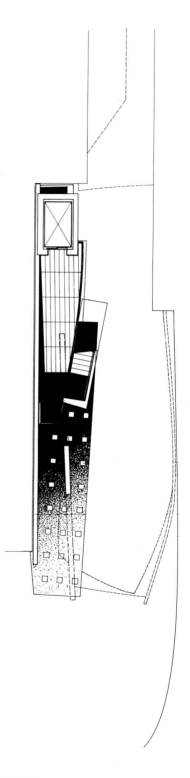

Basement plan

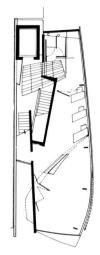

First-floor plan

Fourth-floor plan

Mezzanine gallery

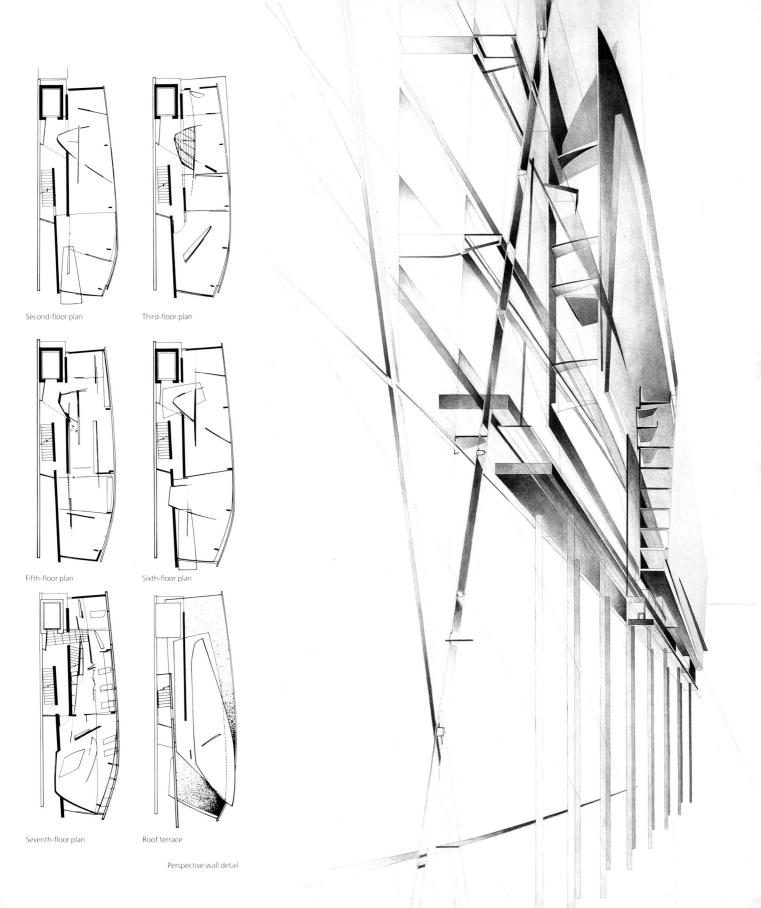

Second-floor plan

Third-floor plan

Fifth-floor plan

Sixth-floor plan

Seventh-floor plan

Roof terrace

Perspective wall detail

IBA **HOUSING**

Berlin, 1986–93

Right from the beginning we had to confront two fundamental issues: the IBA strategy of infill and repair and the tight building regulations for social housing, which contradict modern open-plan layouts. In addition to these constraints were the surrounding buildings, which represented a wide range of different types and periods, so despite guidelines stipulating that new developments in the area must contain an average of five storeys, a seamless insertion into this erratic context would have been virtually impossible.

We therefore interpreted the five-storey planning restriction by creating a long three-storey block that terminated in an eight-storey tower at the corner. The longer block's lower floors contain commercial premises with standardized dwellings above; on top is a roof garden with a children's playground. The sculpted tower, clad in anodized sheet metal, contains three wedge-shaped lofts on each floor.

Worm's-eye view

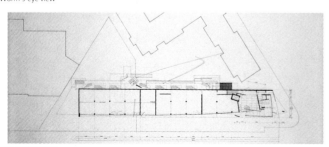

Ground-floor plan

Second-floor plan

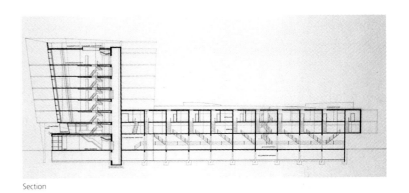
Section

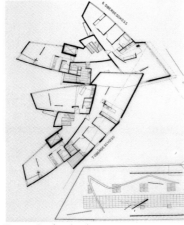

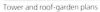
Tower and roof-garden plans

Perspective view

Combined plans and sections for Azabu-Jyuban and Tomigaya

AZABU-JYUBAN

Tokyo, 1986

Drawing on the experiences of the Ku'Damm project in 1986 [p. 34], we realized the great potential for releasing space. In Tokyo – Blade Runner territory – most sites are beyond the boundaries of space, and many buildings only increase the city's stifling congestion.

Slicing into the landscape and piercing the earth, the building exaggerates the pressure of its narrow site in a canyon of random buildings near the Roppongi district. The pristine glass structure is compressed between a tall metal wall and a reinforced concrete wall punctured by jewel-like windows. Between the walls are two curtain walls – one of blue glass, the other clear – that tilt out, rising to the terrace's parapet walls. Inside, the full impact of the released space is immediately apparent in the three-storey entrance space. A vertical stairway runs from the building's heart all the way up to the top, exploding into dramatic balconies.

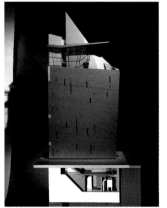

Study models

TOMIGAYA

Tokyo, 1986

This small mixed-use project in a cluttered residential area is related in several respects to Azabu-Jyuban [opposite], but the concept here is inverted. Composed as a series of suspended horizontal spaces and vertical elements that are interlocked by the spiralling motion of stairs and platforms, it is a building in which the volume becomes the void, rather than compressing the void out, as at

Azabu-Jyuban. The centrepiece of the design is a delicate elevated glass pavilion, open on three sides, that hovers above open ground. Most of the building is below the curving ground floor, which is pulled back from the edges and holds a tall glass wall that allows light into the lower space, whose generous proportions make them flexible for retail and office activities.

In such a dense city, light and air are valuable commodities. We must release these spaces from their constricted sites and breathe light and air into the urban condition.

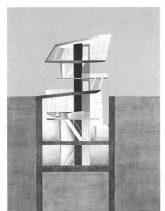

Section

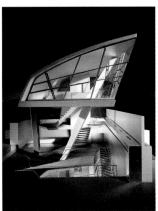

Study model showing glass pavilion

WEST HOLLYWOOD CIVIC CENTRE

Los Angeles, 1987

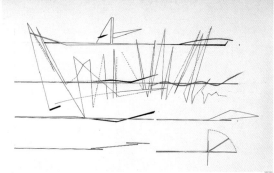

Preliminary studies

There were several interesting challenges in the brief for this design. The first was the relatively young and progressive municipality that sought to make its mark within the patchwork of Los Angeles's complex urban layout. The second was the area's fertile creative resources: West Hollywood has one of the highest concentrations of interior and graphic designers in the country, a fact symbolized by Cesar Pelli's 'Blue Whale', one of the city's most recognizable architectural landmarks; the site for the civic centre was adjacent to it.

The relatively context-free environment brought about one of my earliest explorations of the building as landscape, while the area's flat terrain allowed us to consider the site as a geometric topography, an approach foreshadowed by projects like La Villette [p. 19]. On this urban geometric canvas, objects float and interact in a way that is only possible in wide-open spaces.

Exploded perspective [above]   Aerial perspective [below]

AL WAHDA SPORTS CENTRE

Abu Dhabi, 1988

In stark contrast to the dense urban projects executed for sites in Berlin and Tokyo [pp. 34–43], the setting for this sports complex allowed us to expand into, rather than compress, the setting. The structure therefore became a large-scale landscape relief, mirroring and settling into the land's contours. To some extent this project marks an early exploration into the landscape. The project comprises three main elements: a podium, conceived as a suspended park that provides access to the stadium and viewing platforms; a new ground plane, which ascends from street level and slips underneath the podium; and the stadium, which rises out of the shifting ground plane and podium and permits various seating arrangements and uses.

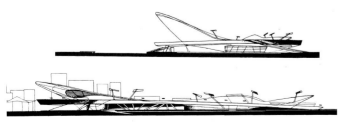

Elevations

METROPOLIS

Institute of Contemporary Arts, London, 1988

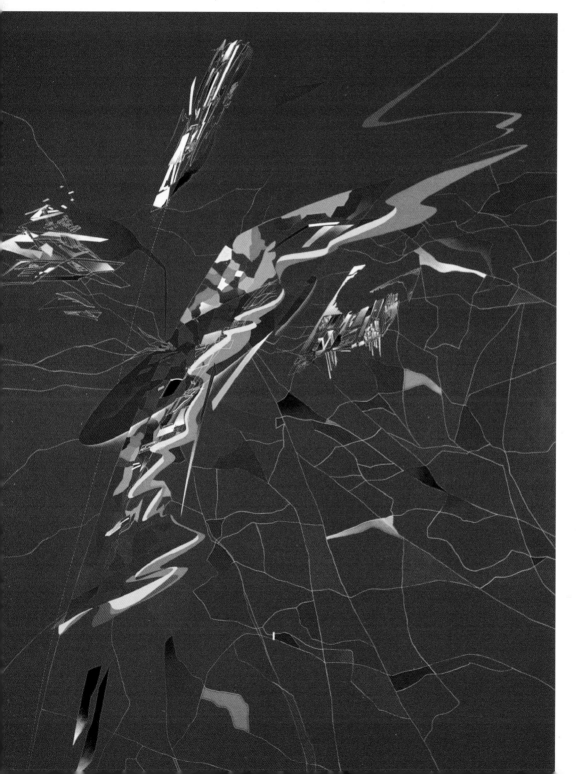

The screaming redness of this painting, commissioned for an exhibition that explored facets of the metropolis, is meant to express an exasperation with the sprawling mess that is London. On one level, the painting shows London as a patchwork of villages. But rather than promoting an even distribution of this urban merging – which has been evolving for centuries – we articulated the city as polycentric, where a number of metropolitan centres condense at different focal points. In this context, the red represents the fires of London, where new settlements and new centres need to be invented to replace an exhausted and overworked heart.

London Metropolis Red Panels

The Dead Zone

BERLIN 2000

1988

Before the collapse of the Wall in 1989, we were invited to speculate about the city's future. As part of an overall scheme between the axes of Mehringplatz to Bahnhof Friedrichstrasse and Brandenburger Tor to Alexanderplatz, the falling of the Wall offered new possibilities for regeneration. We considered both the expansion and the repair of the city, ranging from corridors of development to 'Wall-zone' building programmes.

The focus of our vision was the Alexanderplatz. Because it represents one of the few attempts to go beyond typical nineteenth-century urbanism, we decided to leave it free of homogeneous commercial development, to stand in poignant contrast to the vulnerable line that used to demarcate Berlin's division. A series of diagrams [right] shows possible development of these newly released territories. Corridor cities project into the landscape, and in the lower diagrams, new geometries inhabit the former dead zone, sometimes rectilinear yet slightly out of sync with the existing order.

In our eyes the Wall zone could become a linear park. Where once a concrete ribbon wall and no-go zone lay, we would lay down a strip of park, decorated with buildings.

47

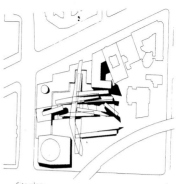

VICTORIA CITY
AREAL

Berlin, 1988

Site plan

Before the Wall came down, this site
epitomized Berlin's state as an urban
island. The site is on a major axis, the
Kurfürstendamm, but completely
enclosed and virtually inaccessible.
To create a building in such a
fortified context suggested that we
should intensify the urban density
horizontally. The site was thus
divided into new air corridors with
three distinct zones that contain the
three major functions, shopping
facilities, offices and a hotel.

Shopping areas

Because the cruciform site would
be the new focus of several major
thoroughfares – streets and rail lines
– a new shopping area is terraced in
concentric relation to the shops on
the fringe of the site. This enclosed
space is glass-floored and is
suspended over further public
facilities, which include more shops,
the hotel lobby, a multipurpose
assembly hall, a conference centre
and a restaurant. Above, an
extendible system of office beams –
each of which might maintain a
distinct corporate identity – is
superimposed on the shopping
facilities. On top of this floats a
bent slab containing the hotel.

Offices

Hotel-related areas

Ground-floor plan

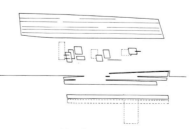

Programmes [above]

Aerial perspective [above left]

Blue Beam [left]

49

A NEW BARCELONA

1989

The diagonal axes of Cerda's nineteenth-century plan for the city's expansion is the pivotal element for our reconstruction of it. Our new urban geometry is based on a subtle twisting of the diagonal into skewed, interlocking fragments. As this field traverses urban contexts, it is constantly intersected by an 'elastic corridor' of local conditions – irregular (village), gridded (housing zones) or strips (railways and waterfront) – that triggers an urban response and multiplies street activity in each neighbourhood.

Early studies

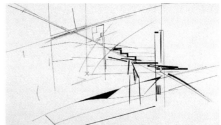

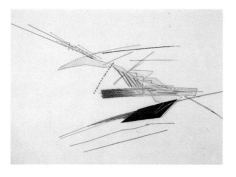

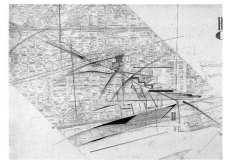

TOKYO FORUM

Tokyo, 1989

Similar to the principles employed in the Azabu-Jyuban and Tomigaya projects [pp. 42–43], this design aims to counteract the congestion of Tokyo. The central form is a void – a glass container – out of which smaller voids are dramatically hollowed and which house the building's cultural and conference areas.

Within a labyrinth of closely knit rooms – like the plan of Pompeii – the conference areas are clustered and separated by variable partitions. At ground level, these spaces can be glimpsed through sharply cut slits in the glass floor. Upper levels contain exhibition spaces, studios, restaurants and public areas. On the roof is a landscaped garden with a diagonal cut that allows light and ventilation into the lower floors.

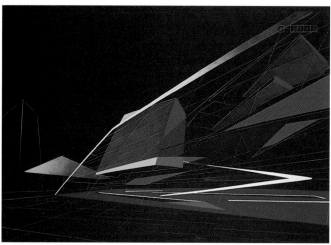

View from plaza

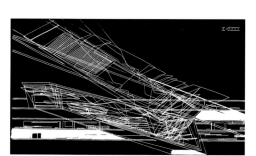

Plan and section of main hall

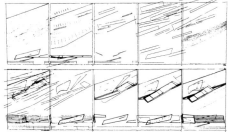

Plan and sections

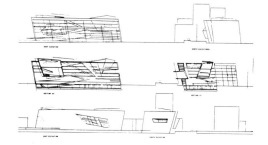

Elevations and sections

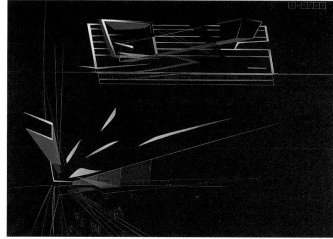

Elevation perspective rotation

Exploded perspective

51

HAFENSTRASSE DEVELOPMENT

Hamburg, 1989

In the old harbour street containing
traditional four- and five-storey
houses were two sites – or rather,
gaps – slated for redevelopment. The
street and its row houses are part of
a series of parallel strips – a small
park, the new street and the
embankment being the other
elements – that step down to the
Elbe. Our objective was to create
links running across the strips and to
transform the embankment into a
recreation area.

One site is located on an acute
corner. A slab building leans forward
and twists back, opening to the
riverfront. The vertical organization
is a sequence of commercial and
residential layers, with a public space
on the first two levels. Sliding

Site study

Corner building rotation

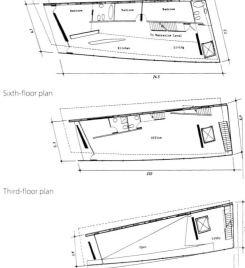

Sixth-floor plan

Third-floor plan

Ground-floor plan

Longitudinal and cross sections

Model [below]

sections of the glass curtain wall enable parts of each floor to become outdoor terraces. The elevation facing the river is a continuous curtain wall that wraps over to become the penthouse roof.

The second site was a gap in the nineteenth-century block. We envisioned a series of compressed slabs that, despite being a dense agglomeration, allowed for a degree of transparency. As one passes the building, gaps open and close between the structure's interstices, defying the notion of a flat façade. The ground floor contains retail spaces; residential units are above, and some connect horizontally across the slabs. Many aspects of this project anticipate the underlying principles of the Art and Media Centre in Düsseldorf [p. 68].

Middle site studies [above]; corner site studies [following pages]

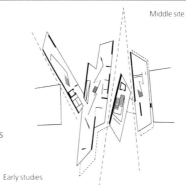

Early studies

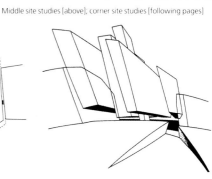

MOONSOON

Sapporo, Japan, 1989–90

For a two-fold programme of formal eating and relaxed lounging we wanted to create an opposition of moods. The result is two synthetic and strange worlds: fire and ice. Inspired by the seasonal ice buildings of Sapporo, the ground floor features cool greys materialized in glass and metal. Tables are sharp fragments of ice; a raised floor level drifts like an iceberg across the space. Above the ice chamber whirls a furnace of fire, rendered in searing reds, brilliant yellows and exuberant oranges. A spiral above the bar tears through the ground-floor ceiling, curling up to the underside of the upper-level dome like a fiery tornado bursting through a pressure vessel. A plasma of biomorphic sofas accommodates eating and lounging and allows an infinite configuration of seating types with movable trays and plug-in sofa backs.

Ground floor

Worm's-eye view of restaurant

Entrance to the Iceberg

Iceberg detail [opposite]

Painting study of Iceberg

56

Orange Peel detail [opposite]

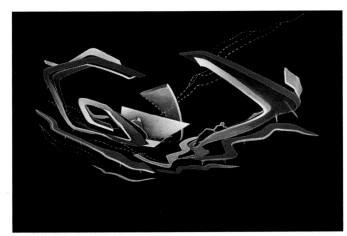
Bar/lounge: view from underneath

Lounge area

Lounge area

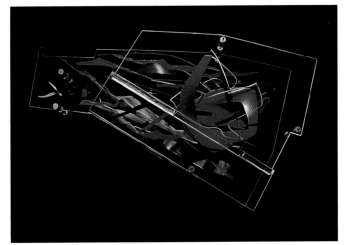
Perspex model

Rotations [above]

Plans/elevations [left]

FOLLY 3

Expo '90, Osaka, 1989–90

Our site at the International Expo in Osaka was located on an open plaza at the junction of several paths. We designed a series of compressed and fused elements to expand in the landscape and refract pedestrian movement. From afar, two vertically extruded planes signal the folly to approaching visitors, while up close horizontal planes define the structure's perimeters and create a series of canyons. Contrasting with the flying planes, five ramps of varying size stretch along the ground plane. The unexpected junctions of these dynamic horizontal and vertical elements create a number of coves, where visitors may seek

temporary refuge from the arduous exercise of walking and sightseeing.

With its bundled and twisting walls, we were also able to treat the Osaka project as a half-scale experiment for the Vitra Fire Station [p. 62].

LEICESTER SQUARE

London, 1990

The idea of designing new fountains
to decorate public places is
redundant. Shoot the square;
it is dead. Hopes of renovating
the existing square should be
abandoned.

We would rather see Leicester
Square as a public room, habitable
and submerged beneath the surface,
a heart that beats with the city. We
would not propose to fill the square
with buildings or spouts of water:
we would turn such structures
upside down and sink them into the
ground. Solid and transparent
skyscrapers slicing into the earth
could contain accommodation, and
water could cascade down these
inverted canyons as a cooling
mechanism for an overworked
heart. Bridges and passages would
traverse the voids and solids of the
new subterranean fabric, while light
slits would remind the visitor of the
city's familiar fabric hovering above.

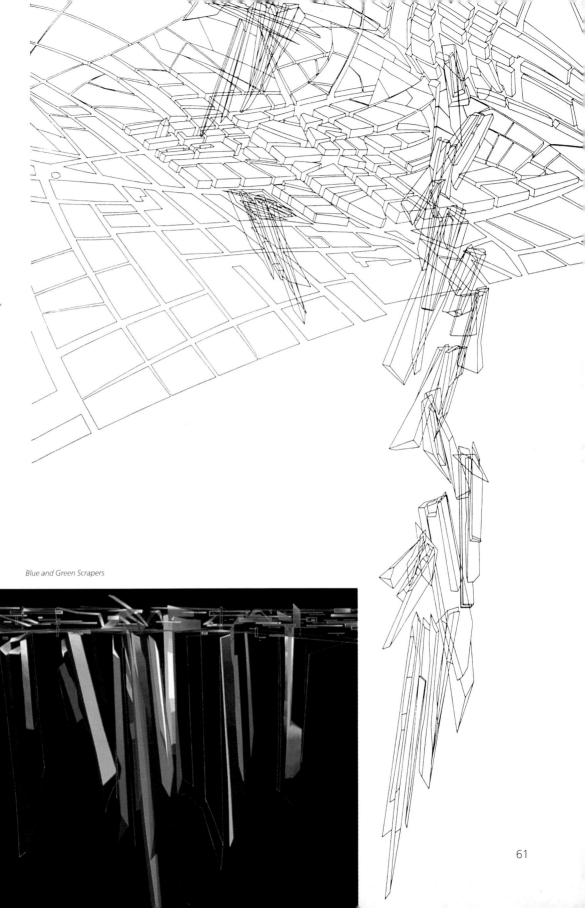

Blue and Green Scrapers

61

VITRA FIRE STATION

Weil am Rhein, Germany, 1990–94

The project began as a commission to build a fire station in the north-east section of the vast Vitra furniture factory complex, as well as design boundary walls, a bicycle shed and other small elements. Because the site already contained a disparate array of large-scale factory buildings, we decided to concentrate on the site as a zone within this industrial landscape that stretched from the main gate to the far end of the site, where the fire station would stand.

The fire station is designed as the edge of this 500-metre-long zone, which itself becomes an artificial landscape. As expansions occur, our scheme allows for a dynamic pattern to develop between the spaces, like furniture in a large room.

The design's primary feature is a series of layered screening walls, between which spaces are punctured and break according to the station's functions. The main

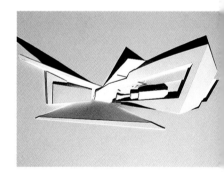

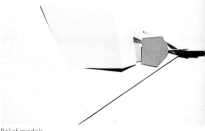

Relief models

puncture is the movement of the fire engines, perpendicular to the line of the walls and the landscape as a whole. As one walks across the structure, the red fire engines are the central focus of this landscape. And as the fire engine's red lines appear to be written on the asphalt, so are the rituals of the firemen inside inscribed like choreographic notation. The whole building is frozen motion, suspending the tension of alertness, ready to explode into action at any moment.

Aerial site plan

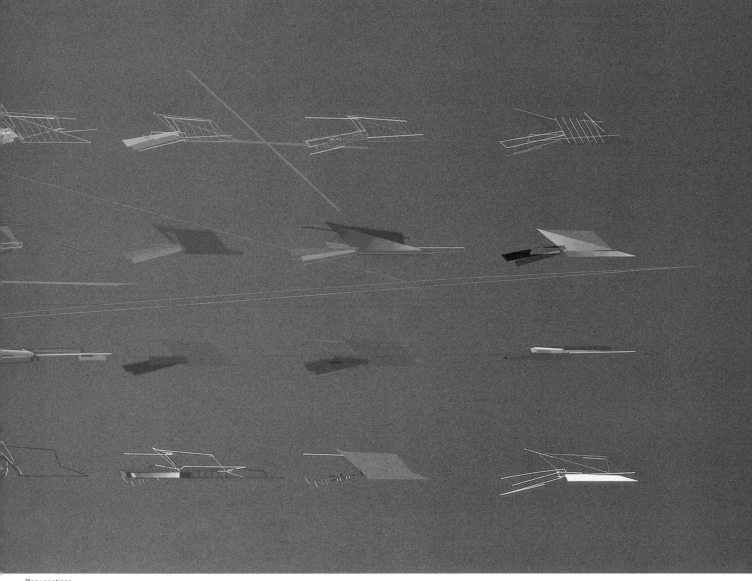

Plan variations

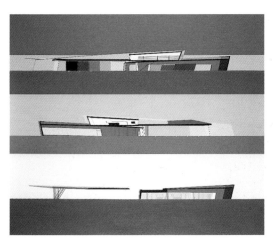

Elevations (dark)

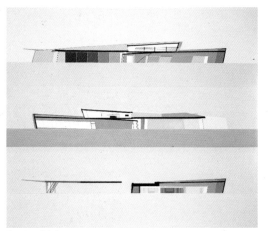

Elevations (light)

ART AND MEDIA CENTRE

Düsseldorf (Rheinhafen), 1989–93

Shadow studies

For the redevelopment of Düsseldorf's prominent harbour into an enterprise zone containing offices for an advertising agency and studios interspersed with shops, restaurants and leisure facilities, we created an artificial landscape that faced the river and became an extension of the water's activities and functions. This landscape is protected by a 90-metre-long wall-like building that contains the offices and blocks out traffic noise.

From the river an enormous metallic triangle cuts into the site, piercing the wall to form an entrance ramp. The adjoining ground planes crack open to reveal technical studios to the north, and shops and restaurants. Below ground, a wall of technical services is compressed, so that part of the wall rises above ground and curves around to create a 320-seat cinema.

The wall's street-side has tiny linear incisions in its concrete; on the river side, levels are articulated by varying depths of cantilever on each floor. A glazed 'finger' building is a fragmented series of slabs set perpendicular to the street like glass splinters that have broken free from the wall. Where the slabs converge, a void is carved out for conference rooms and exhibition areas.

A minimalist glass box surrounded by a family of sculpted feet and heavy triangular structures, the entrance lobby is at the intersection of the wall and the finger building. From here the street and riverscape are visually connected. A ribbonlike grand stair leads up to the conference rooms through the underbelly of a heavy slab suspended above.

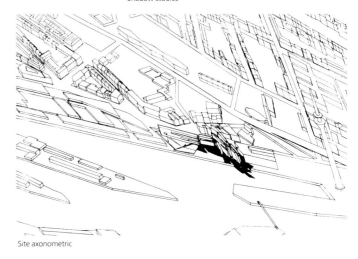

Site axonometric

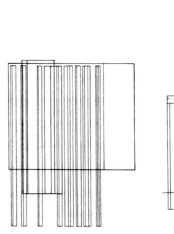

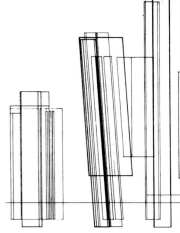

Perspex models [below]

Agency core rotation [above]

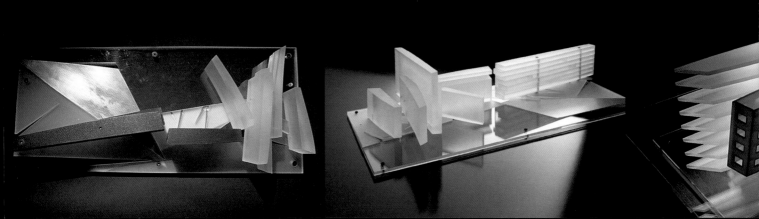

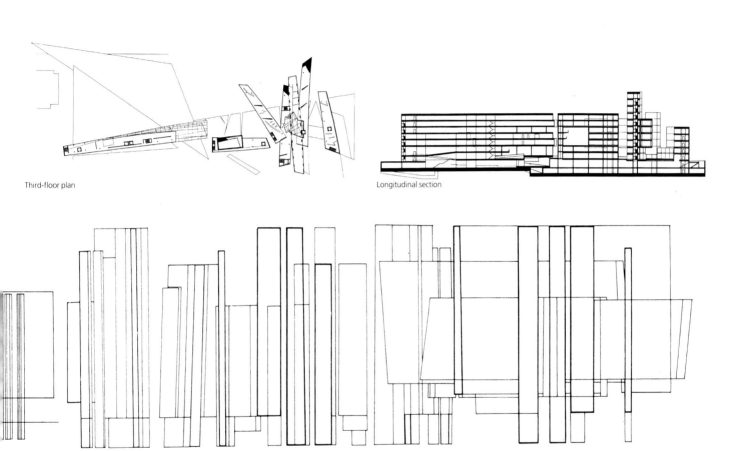

Third-floor plan

Longitudinal section

Landscape perspective rotation painting [following pages]

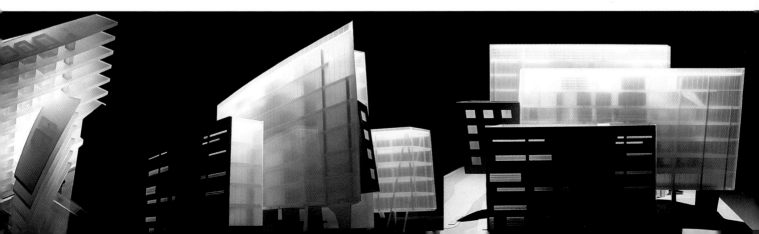

MUSIC VIDEO PAVILION

Groningen, The Netherlands, 1990

The intention for our music-video pavilion was to make a playful place in what was for me the most challenging location in the city: the gap between the monumental A-kerk and the Korenbeurs buildings in the Vismarkt district. Like the 'monitor' houses of New York's Fire Island – clapboard houses with huge plate-glass windows facing the ocean, which at night reveal lofty interiors – the design for this pavilion provides a window to the world in which people can be seen moving amid video imagery, becoming part of the performance.

Trapped between two walls set one metre apart are decks which protrude into the glazed enclosure. Images are projected from the upper decks onto the mid-deck, onto translucent panels set into the glazed façade and onto the raised-

Detail of orange balcony

72

Alternative proposal: plans, elevations, sections,
elevations and structural frames [below]

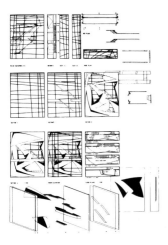

Main façade at night [below]   Study models

Rear window

ground finish beneath. It takes a lot
of money and effort to produce
short video-slices of message and
song, but the videos are insufficient
on their own. We wanted film-
makers, performers and video
producers to have a structure with
which they could experiment.

HOTEL AND RESIDENTIAL COMPLEX

Abu Dhabi, 1990

Like many American cities, Abu Dhabi is organized on a grid. As a uniform structure the grid serves as the basis against which special architectural 'events' are placed. For a hotel complex located on a prime site in the city centre, we flipped up this horizontal urban grid to become a vertical plane, a slab of apartments and hotel rooms that become a backdrop for hotel-related

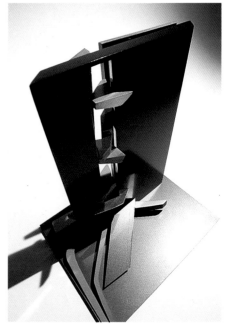

Study models

74

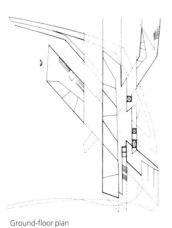

Ground-floor plan

Level-20 plan

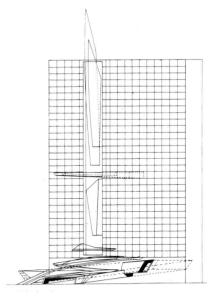

Main elevation

spaces like conference rooms, restaurants and a health club. Where the slab splits apart, these spaces are suspended and sculpted in a 'vertical courtyard'. At ground level a four-storey beam cuts across the site and through the slab, providing spaces for a shopping mall below and offices above. On the beam's fourth floor, with views over the gulf, is the hotel lobby, whose vehicle access is via a curved ramp that swoops from one corner of the site, around the slab and into the vertical courtyard.

INTERZUM 91

Gluzendorf, Germany, 1990

We were asked by a German timber manufacturer to create an exhibition stand to display their products for the biannual Interzum trade show. The primary intention of our design was to create a separate environment that could be experienced on several levels. Within

the backdrop of a large and sterile trade show, we wanted to induce the sense of an insolated landscape within an enclosed structure. Inside, a central pathway, which, like the trunk of a tree, had branches that ran off it, led to product exhibits and ambient surroundings.

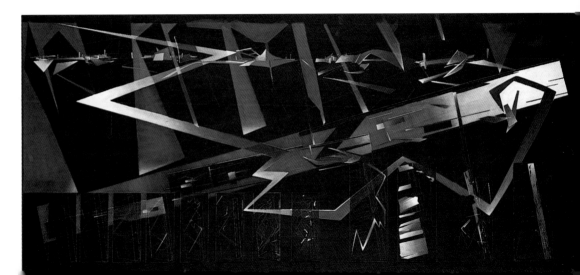

LONDON 2066

Vogue Magazine (U.K.), 1991

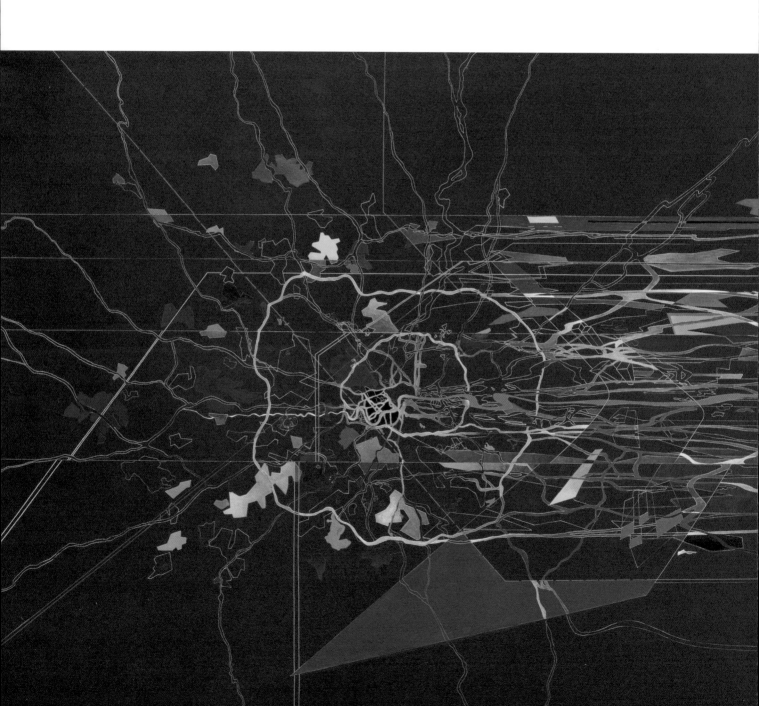

This large-scale painting continues the exploration of views into London's urban character that began with the Grand Buildings project [p. 25], *Metropolis* [p. 46] and the fountains project for Leicester Square [p. 61]. This work presents our most radical shake-up of the metropolis in both diagrammatic and pictorial terms within a single painting – and it should be judged by this radicalness. We studied plans of the open spaces, rail, road, water and air routes and borough layout and restructured the entire plan. As the brush moves over London from the west, strands converge, stretch and continue – not always in parallel – towards the east. These strokes cut new section-lines of air and area for what we believe could be new areas for buildings, for it is the very intersection of vertical structures to the ground where public activities would be intensified in this new plan.

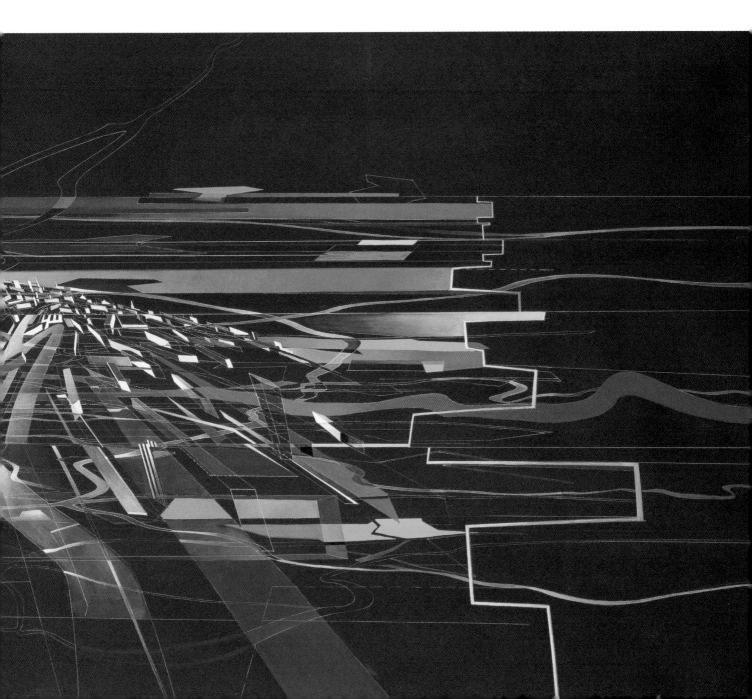

THE HAGUE VILLAS

Hague Housing Festival,
The Hague, 1991

The single-family house is a building type that continues to be constrained by convention. We presented two designs as part of a 'field' of eight villas to be located in a suburb of The Hague. The two villas, to be constructed of reinforced concrete, abstract the conventional configuration of domestic spaces to create unexpected spatial and social interactions.

The first design – the 'cross house' – is formed from a ground-level podium that is intersected by two 'beams' that enclose most of the residence. The lower beam is cut into the podium level, a 'negative' space that forms a courtyard. The upper beam is 'positive', housing an open living and studio space that floats above the podium and crosses the courtyard. The house is thus a superimposition of two opposite living conditions – introverted and extroverted.

Study models

Top view of cross house

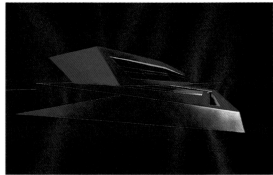

Cross-house painting

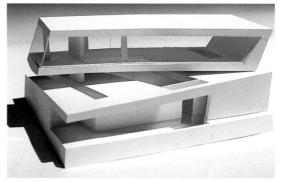

Cross-house model

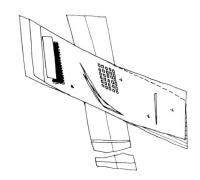

Cross-house sketch

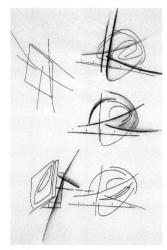

Sketches

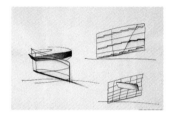

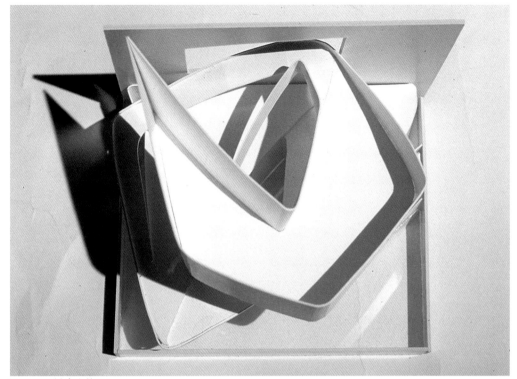

Prototype model of spiral house

The 'spiral house' is essentially a cube through which a floor plate revolves from the entrance level up through the living areas to an upper-level studio, occasionally poking through the exterior. Glazed façades follow the floor's spiral, describing a rotation that is alternately solid, louvred, translucent and, finally, transparent. Residual spaces and gaps between the interstices of the exterior and internal spiral afford surprising views and channels of communication and interaction.

Spiral-house section

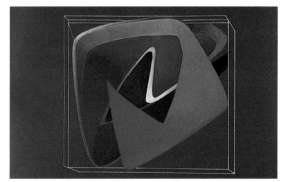

Top view of spiral-house painting

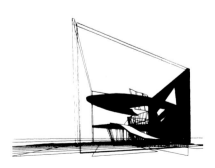

Ground-level perspective of spiral house

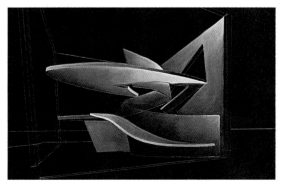

Spiral-house painting

79

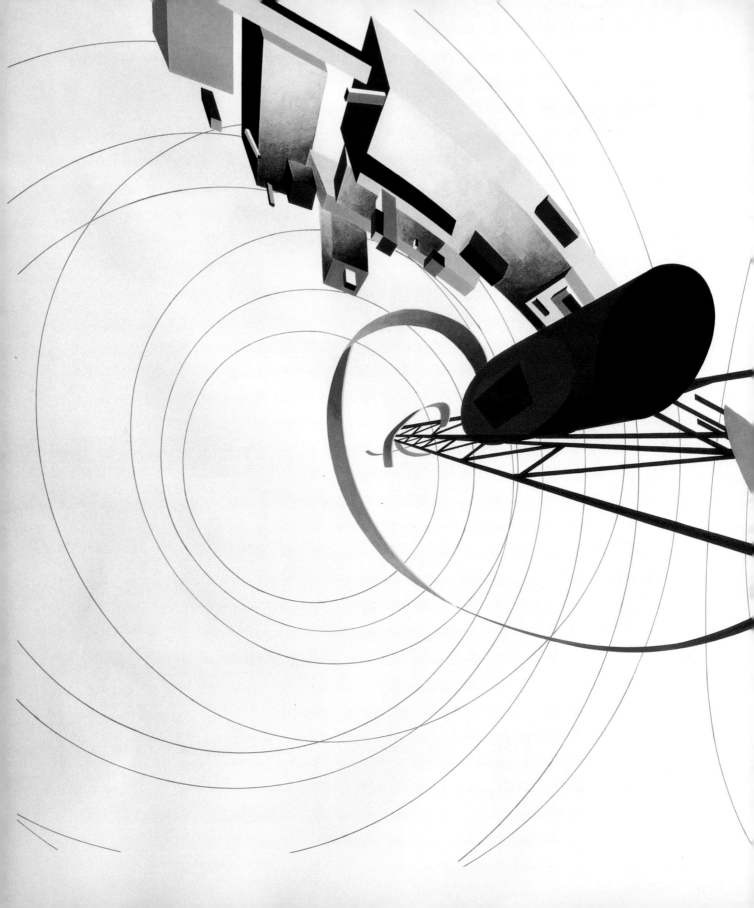

THE GREAT UTOPIA

Solomon R. Guggenheim Museum,
New York, 1992

Tektonik [preceding pages]

The design for an exhibition on Russian Suprematism and Constructivism offered the opportunity to revisit my student explorations of the three-dimensional qualities of Malevich's tektonik [p. 16]. Our proposal for the Guggenheim show featured two large-scale installations of the Tatlin Tower and Malevich's Tektonik, which both engaged in their own ways with Frank Lloyd Wright's spiralling form and were in turn distorted by the space. For the first time, Malevich's tektonik was habitable: visitors had to pass through it to reach the upper galleries.

Our design for the galleries features interventions that actively engage with the objects on display. For example, the tower and tektonik set up the opposition between Malevich's *Red Square* and Tatlin's *Corner Relief*. For the space containing work from the original *0.10* exhibition, one of Malevich's

Tatlin Tower

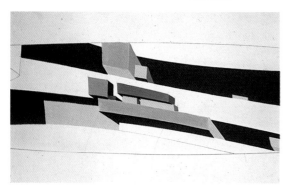

Bent Tektonik

Suprematist compositions has been extruded from the floor. In the Black Room, which shows objects from the 1921 *5 x 5 = 25* exhibition, paintings displayed on Perspex stands appear to dematerialize and float above the floor. This sense of weightlessness is encountered again in the Globe Room, in which constructions hanging from the ceiling gravitate towards a white orb that emerges from the floor.

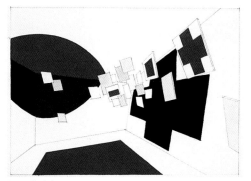

Storm of Paintings

0.10 Storm

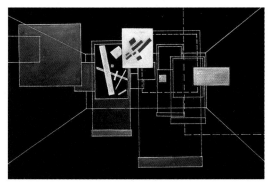

Black Room: 5 x 5 = 25

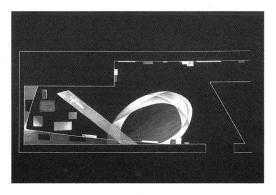

Globe Room

VISION FOR MADRID

1992

Historically, the growth of Madrid could be described as a successive bursting of shells: the circular medieval city, the nineteenth-century grid and, in the twentieth century, the linear development now defined by a highway in the form of an ellipse. Framed in the west by the Rio Manzanares, the city is now growing mainly eastwards. Suburbs of housing blocks have mushroomed beyond the M30 highway and are about to engulf the nearby villages.

Our objective was to prevent the city from collapsing into formless-ness, to channel and organize this anarchic spread of development. We proposed four specific areas of redevelopment and regeneration. To the south, the former industrial fabric around the city's railways could be transformed into lively parks and leisure-landscapes; new commercial development could be

concentrated along the strip-corridor leading to the airport; the north–south axis, Paseo de Castellana, could be intensified by inserting buildings into existing slivers and public spaces into open pockets; and, finally, the remaining gaps in the suburbs should be preserved.

Relief model

Painting study of linear expansion

BILLIE STRAUSS HOTEL

Nabern, Germany, 1992

The context for this art-hotel addition was an interesting one: a half-timbered farmhouse and stable that the clients wanted to augment with a challenging new structure that would have a sculptural presence. The heart of the design is a 'blobby', an elliptical space that mediates between the old building and the new one. Partly set into the foundation, the space can be used for performances or exhibitions. In the tower above this lively pivot point are three levels of rooms based on the cross and star, each of which

South elevation

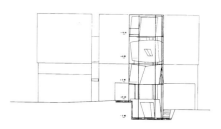

West elevation

Model

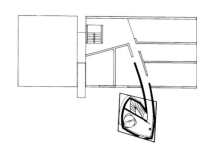

Second-floor plan

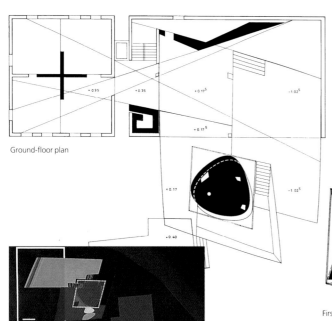

Ground-floor plan

has a completely self-contained environment with built-in furniture and fittings. A third motif, the spiral, is shared by the two other spaces as they connect back to the main building. In a village of strong local character, the ensemble sets up a striking contrast, one that is intended to encourage debate and creativity.

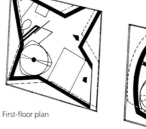

First-floor plan

Second-floor plan

Third-floor plan

Painting of elements

CONCERT HALL

Copenhagen, 1992–93

This large structure achieves both compactness and openness by striking deep cuts of light, land and water through a solid volume that occupies a compact site. These sharp cuts are open to the sky, and show the full relief of the hall. A curved diagonal cut cleaves off the public-square component, bringing the promenade slowly up into the building. Sculpturally expressive volumes of the structure, articulated by different colours of granite, compress space between them. The structures are made from cast-in-place reinforced concrete to allow irregularly shaped flat slabs to be formed.

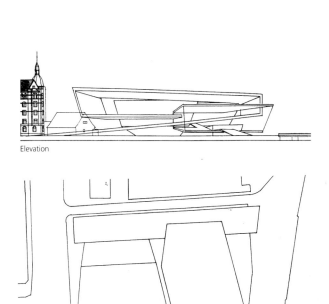

Elevation

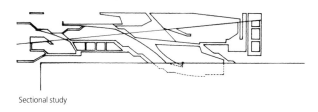

Sectional study

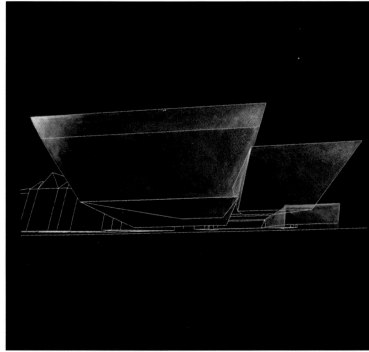

Perspective painting

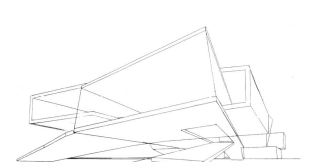

Site plan

Ground-level perspective

RHEINAUHAFEN REDEVELOPMENT

Cologne, 1992

Painting of isometric with city context

To connect this former industrial zone to Cologne we used three distinct formal devices – trapezoid, wedge and spiral – to define and adapt the multipurpose site to its heterogeneous surroundings. The shapes are massive, ambiguous entities that are scaled somewhere between buildings and land forms. Working together, the sections form a coherent area with a high density of cultural, leisure, housing and commercial facilities, as well as incorporating old buildings with converted uses and new structures.

The trapezoidal area embraces the

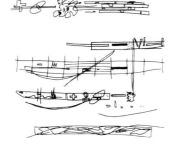

Sketches

entire harbour basin, with two quayside buildings that contain boating facilities and a check-in centre for the riverboat; an area to the north includes a conference centre. Between the trapezoid and

wedge areas rise slanting office towers. The wedge section itself cuts from the banks of the River Rhine into the Ubierring, connecting the riverfront with the Severins housing quarter. Housing is organized in long horizontal blocks on stilts like the former warehouses, as if they have been lifted to allow unobstructed views of the river. The spiral links the Römerpark with the quayside, spanning part of the riverside road. Throughout the site new cultural centres were envisioned as scattered jewels that would reflect the water's movement as it flows by and changes with the seasons.

Study plan of Cologne

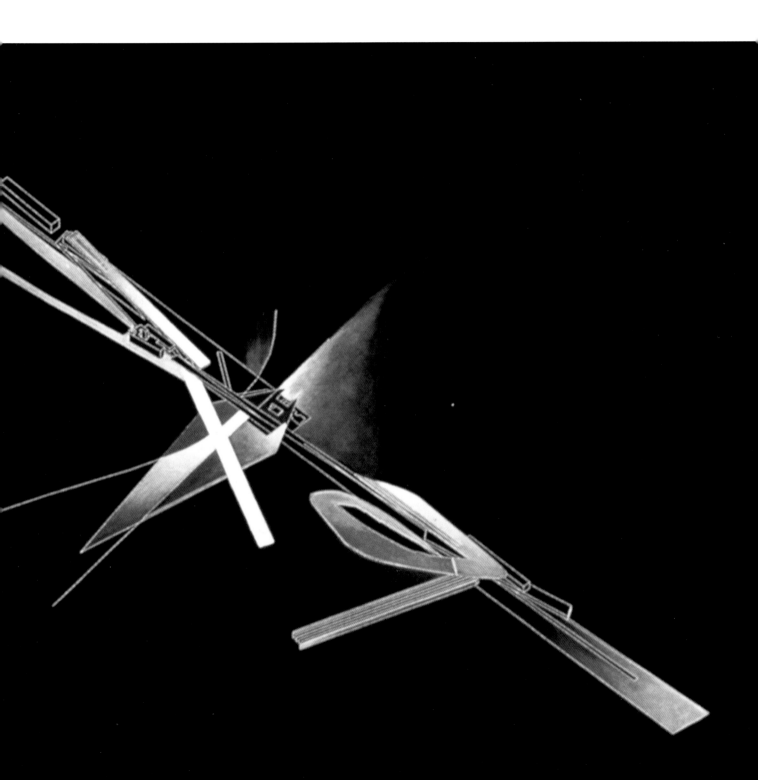

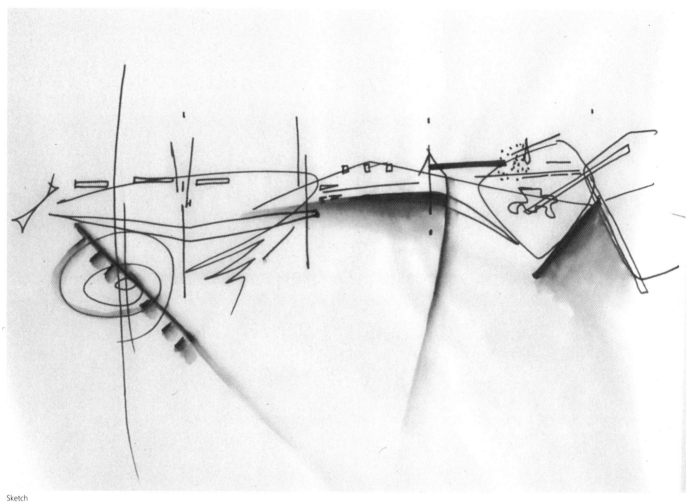

Sketch

Models

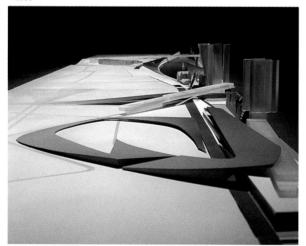 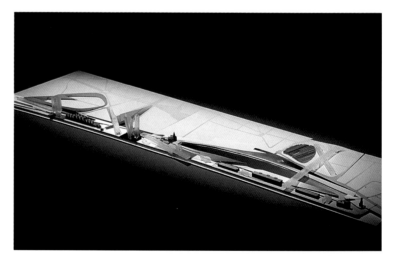

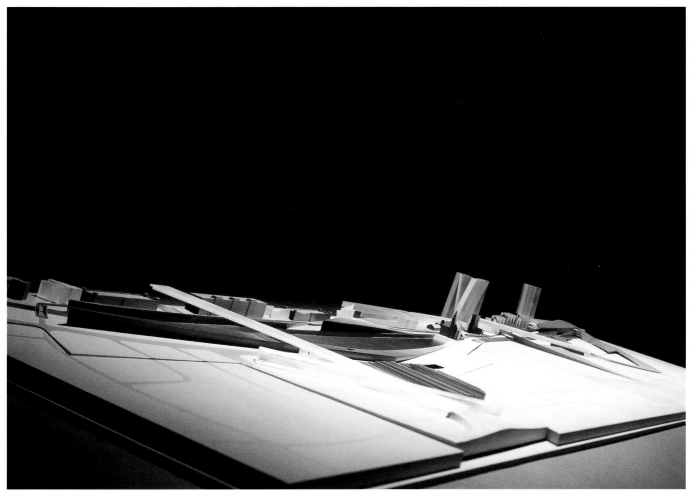

Model

Site plan

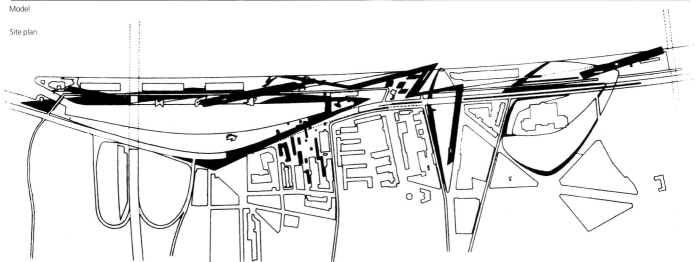

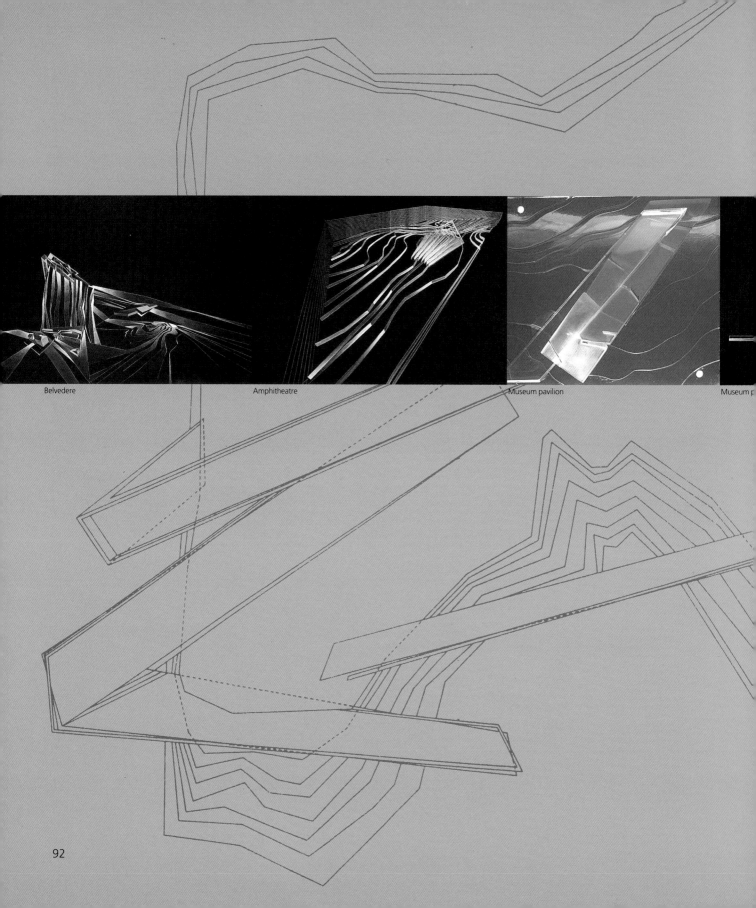

Belvedere

Amphitheatre

Museum pavilion

Museum p

CARNUNTUM

Vienna, 1993

In collaboration with Patrik Schumacher

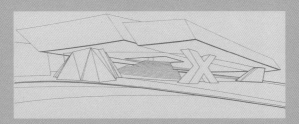

Museum [above and below]

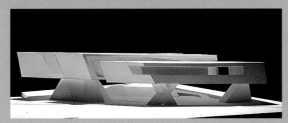

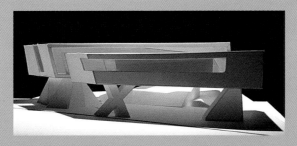

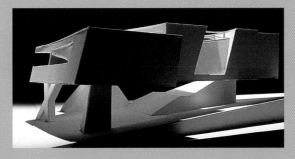

One of the fascinations of archaeological sites is the way in which the remains of human civilization have merged into the landscape and seem at one with nature. In this vein, we wanted the architecture of this cultural park to become another man-made extension of the landscape. We took clues from the geological formations and from local human interventions like quarrying. The buildings – a geological centre, outdoor theatre, belvedere and museum – are the first fragments of a new culture on the mountain that over time will gradually inhabit the surrounding quarry, fragments that suggest an archaeology in reverse.

The geological centre is housed in the history of the mountain itself, its progenitor, cutting into the strata like a blade, revealing the bedrock and thus becoming part of the exhibition. Floors slant against each other like faulted planes; one cuts slices into the mountain, the other follows its slope. The outdoor theatre is conceived as a Greek amphitheatre, a 'found object' in the quarry that follows the earth's contours. Out of this negative, carved space emerges a positive projection, cantilevering over the slope and crystallizing itself over time out of the site's plateau, a natural extension of man-made topography. The museum is the intersection of the concepts explored in the other three projects. The ground plane erupts and thrusts large slabs up into the air, like geological outcroppings. From the street this formation is seen against the mountain, which now has a dialogue with the quarry – the place of the sanctuary – in the distance.

Site-plan painting of landscape

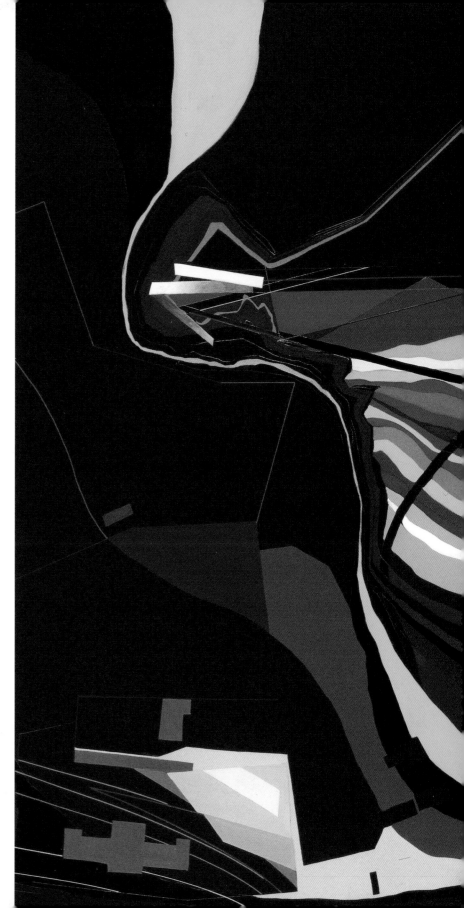

Landscape study painting

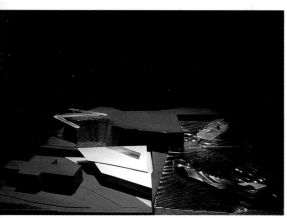

Model

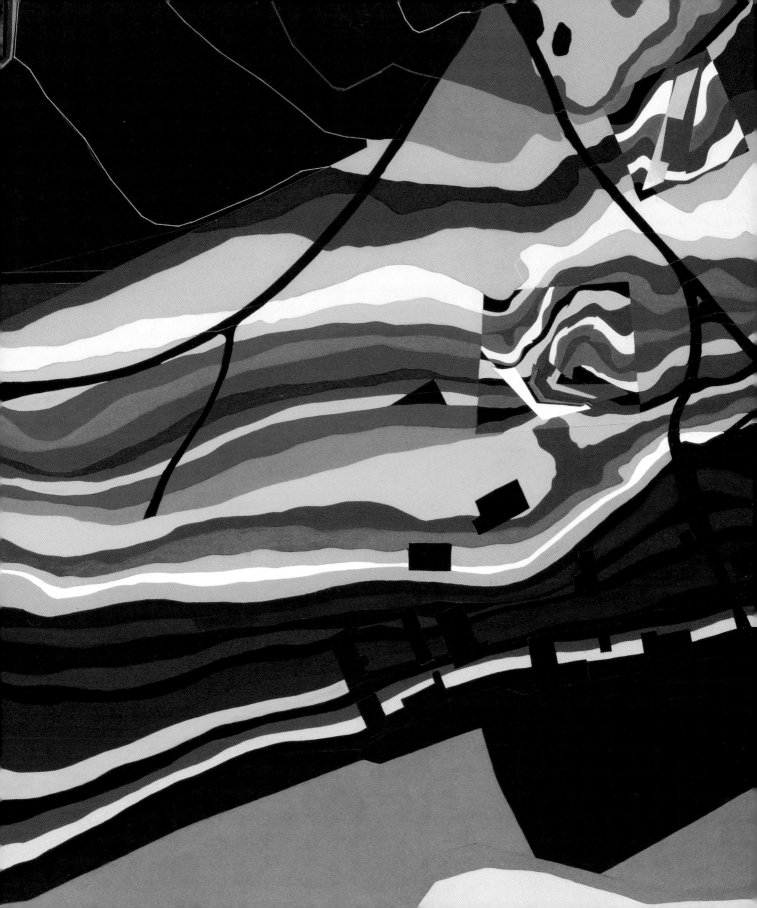

SPITTELAU VIADUCTS

Vienna, 1994–

The project revitalizes a waterfront area in Vienna by linking the water's edge to the city fabric through an existing former railway viaduct. Located along the Donaukanal in Vienna, a series of artists' studios, offices and commercial spaces weave like a ribbon through, around and over the arched bays of the viaduct, designed by Otto Wagner. Shops, cafés and restaurants on the ground floor of three separate buildings cater to the riverfront pedestrian path, which also leads to a nightclub in the old subway tunnel adjacent to the viaduct. The entire project is linked to the university by a pedestrian/cycle bridge.

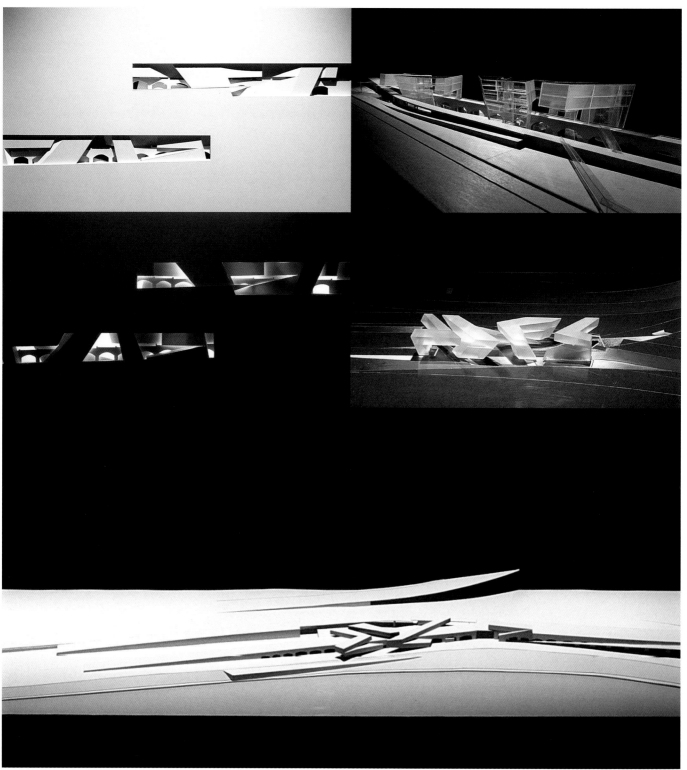

Relief and study models

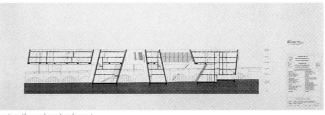

Section through embankment

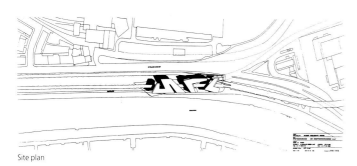

Site plan

Section through viaduct

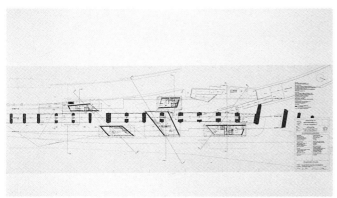

Ground-level plan

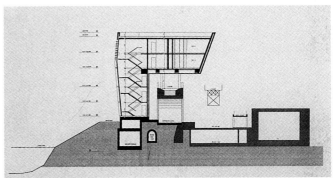

Cross section through Building 1

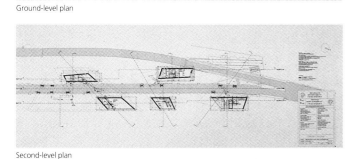

Second-level plan

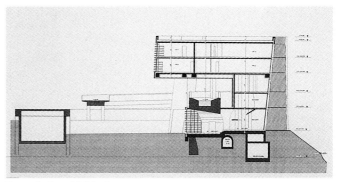

Cross section through Building 2

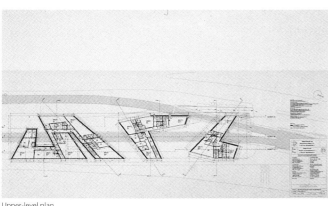

Upper-level plan

Aerial view with nightclub

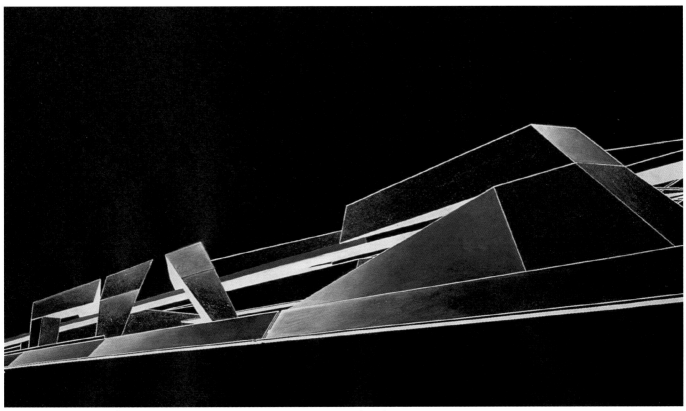

Perspective painting

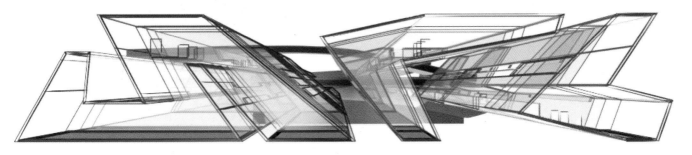

Wire-frame renderings

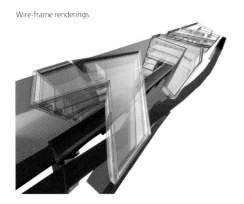

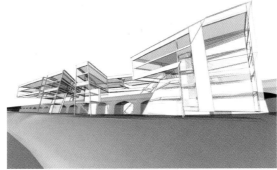

SPITTALMARKT

Berlin, 1995

In collaboration with Patrik Schumacher

The centre of former East Berlin's Mitte is one of the busiest and biggest redevelopment sites in Europe, a forest of cranes and partially erected structures. We were asked to design an office development along one of the district's busiest thoroughfares, the Leipzigerstraße, at a major junction – not unlike the scenario presented to us in the West Berlin Victoria development [p. 49]. The building would contain both the headquarters of a major financial institution and private office spaces.

Our design attempts to mediate between the historic nineteenth-century buildings and the characterless post-War buildings that dominated the skyline before the Wall's collapse. Using an iteration of L-shapes that are collided and woven together, the building consists of three primary slabs that recall the Düsseldorf project [p. 68]. Like the swarming traffic intersection at which they stand, the building's monolithic structures mirror their surroundings while picking up and accentuating the dynamism of the passing cars.

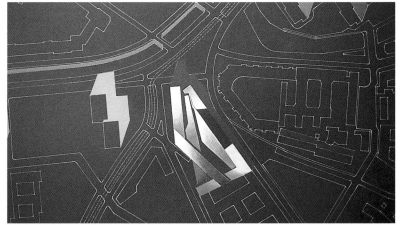
Site plan

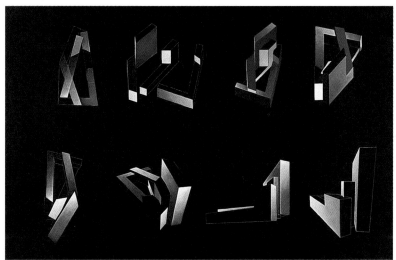
Rotational studies

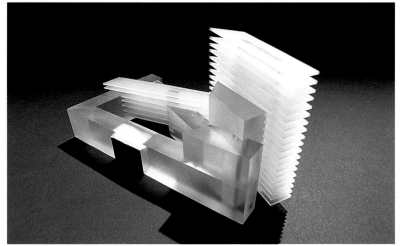
Study model

Street-level perspective

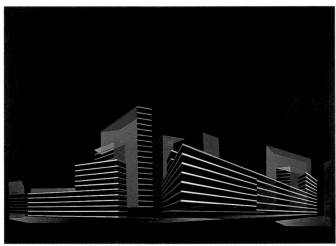

Rotations

LYCEE FRANÇAIS
CHARLES DE GAULLE

London, 1995

The owners of a lycée in South Kensington requested a gatehouse and porter's quarters to mark the entrance to the small existing building and its courtyard. We decided to rotate the traditional vertical gate so that it could be merged with the house on a floating horizontal plane. One passes freely through this building through a forest of column systems, just as one would pass through a gate. The raised horizontal plane is then shattered into puzzle-like segments, each of which is supported by its own structural system of columns, fins and podia, transforming the ground level

Perspective drawings

into a playground of structural elements. In addition to living quarters for the porter and his family, the building contains four classrooms.

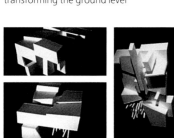

Study models

Sections

Perspectives

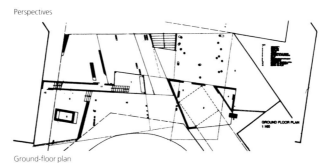

Ground-floor plan

104

PANCRAS LANE

London, 1996

Because of the historic background of London's financial district, designing an office development on a tight site came with a number of planning and building restrictions. The most pertinent was that the ground-floor level must include a public area off the street that functioned as a kind of interior park. We resolved this issue by creating a building that wraps its structure around an area to create an 'outdoor room'. Within the permitted envelope of the site, the 'snake' establishes a balance between indoor and outside space, private office space and public plaza, while introducing a dynamic interaction into the traditional architecture of the City.

Perspective painting

Volumetric rotations

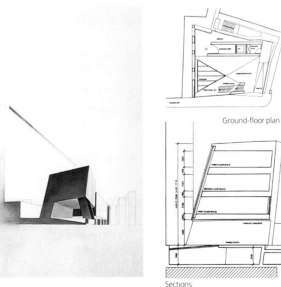

Perspective paintings

Ground-floor plan

Second-floor plan

Sections

42ND STREET HOTEL

New York, 1995

Our design for a hotel complex at the intersection of 8th Avenue at 42nd Street was motivated by a desire to create a microcosm of urbanity that asserted the intricacy and magic of a global city. The proposed complex comprises two three-level commercial podia and two hotels, forty-five floors on the north side and twenty-two floors on the south. Circulation systems, kinetic signage, lighting schemes and the synergy of related entertainment and retail activities unify the complex.

The hotel tower is a vertical street – a tower of towers, stacked in the geometric plan of the square and containing 950 rooms. Each 'building element' contains slightly different rooms and façades. A void through the tower's centre is interrupted by elements of the second tower. Where the hotel tower connects to the commercial podium below, the vertical street spills out into the horizontal plane, into a network of retail shops, restaurants and public hotel facilities, integrating itself into the city's complex plan down to the subway concourse below.

View through void (model)

Façade detail (model)

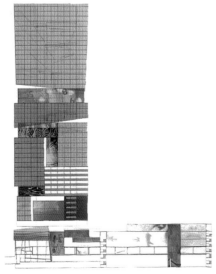

Section

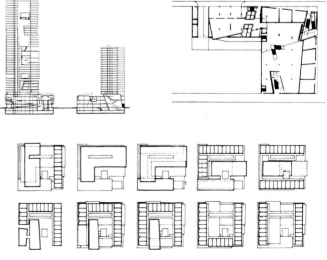

Section and typical upper-level plans

Computer study

Perspective interior view

BLUEPRINT PAVILION

Interbuild 95, Birmingham, England, 1995

The pavilion's form was designed as a continuous and unified space that expressed the circulation of visitors while unifying the products on display within the structure. The structure is defined by a continuous plate that folds into itself to create two interlocking beams so that the inside of the plate becomes the exhibition area. The plate comprises a chassis of steel beams sandwiched between an external cladding material (sheet aluminium or industrial siding) and an internal cladding material (MDF, industrial flooring or other finish). With this arrangement, finishes can flow uninterrupted from the floor to around the walls. Lighting is recessed into the plate or suspended from it.

As a whole, the Möbius-strip-like plate functions as a completely integrated exhibition space. Each exhibitor (in this case, different manufacturers of bathroom fixtures, tables and storage cabinets, carpeting and steel) has a specific location within the 'object', while displayed surface materials – like the floor and wall finish – move seamlessly across one space and into another.

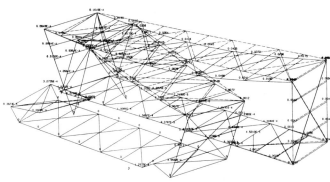

Structural analysis

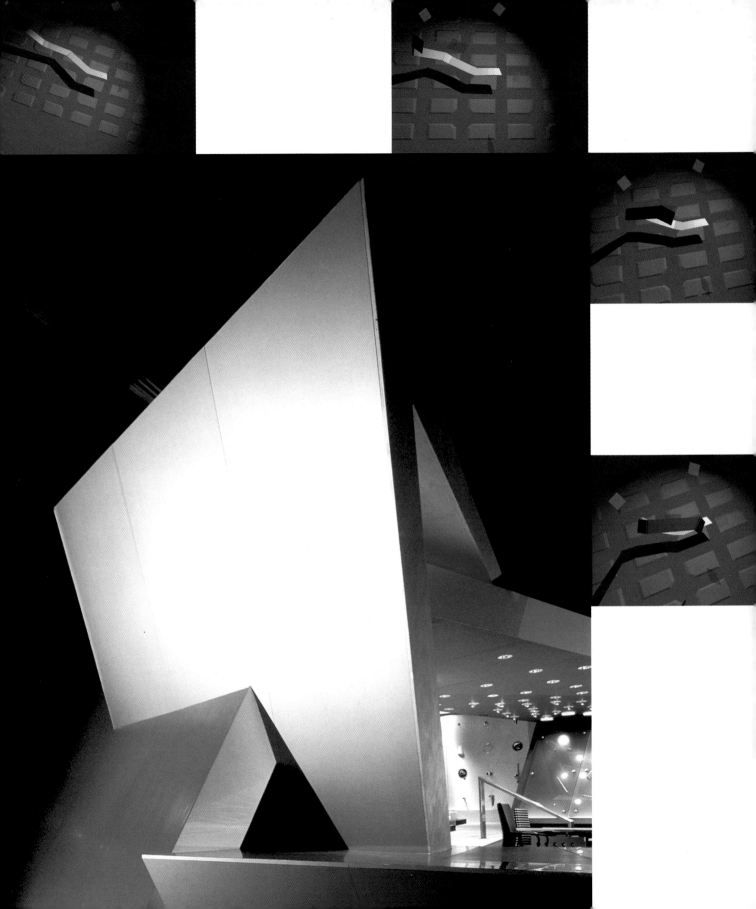

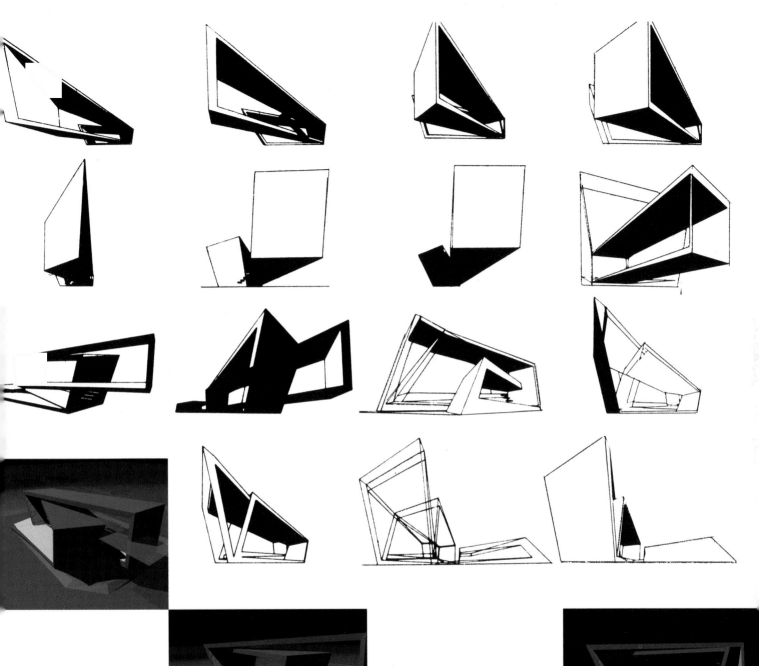

PRADO MUSEUM EXTENSION

Madrid, 1996

The various museums that constitute the Prado are interwoven by an urban calligraphy, architectural inscriptions in the form of embankments, staircases and walls that make up the topography around them – a landscape rather than a building, a twisted ribbon of cultural events in the urban fabric. Our addition to the Prado occurs at the focus and crossing point of the movements through the Prado complex, the point at which this ribbon compresses and curls into a tight wedge behind the Villanueva building. As a natural extension of this ribbon, the new building turns upon itself, generating a continuous flow of interlocking spaces. A wide ramp carves deep into the ground and establishes a new main entrance at basement level. New foyer

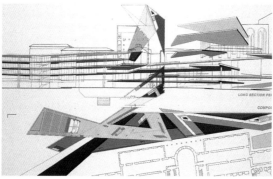

Composite painting of site plan and sections

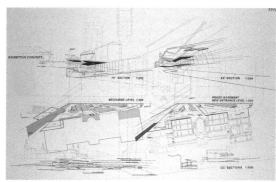

Composite drawings of plan and sections

spaces and ancillary zones are illuminated by light wells that articulate the structure, and temporary exhibition spaces rise above the foyer on two crossing levels. As the ribbon penetrates the end of the site's wedge, it flips into a vertical strip containing offices, ateliers and conservation studios.

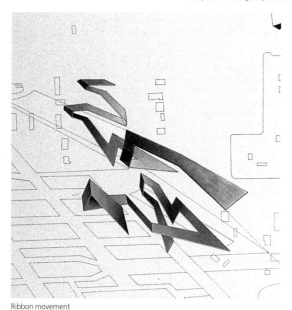

Ribbon movement

Rotation painting

CARDIFF BAY OPERA HOUSE

Cardiff, Wales, 1994–96

Exploded aerial view painting [right]
Perspective from Pierhead Street [below]
Perspective from oval basin [bottom]

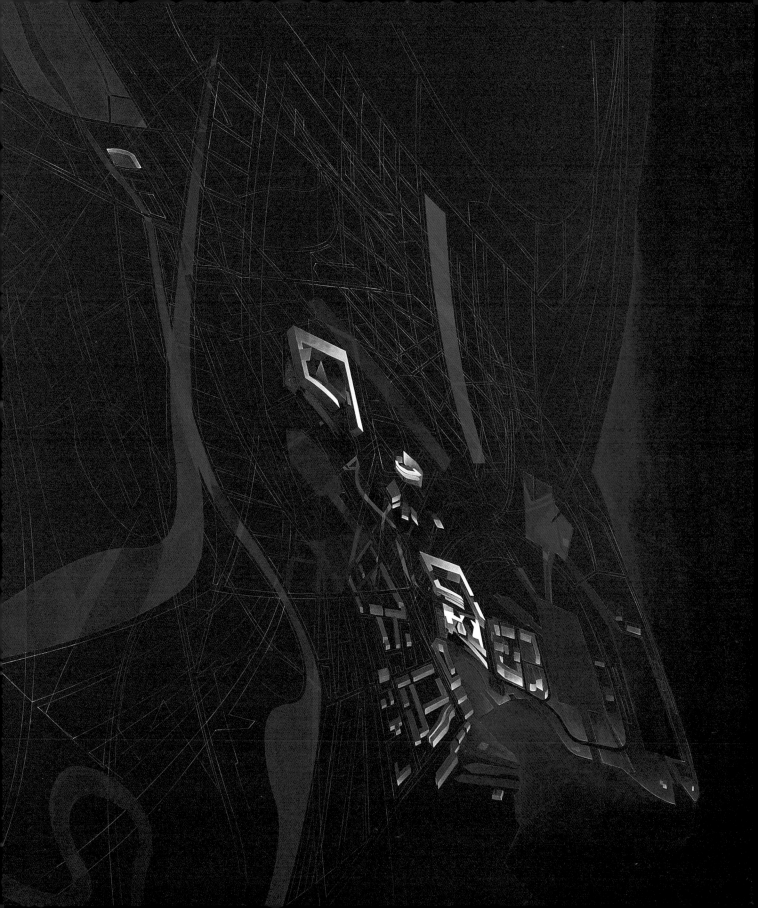

For the new home of the Welsh National Opera we wanted to create a 'living-room' for the city, a building that extended the public spaces of this port city into a symbol of urban pride. The primary device to achieve this effect and to embrace the activities of the complex while creating its own context was a glazed perimeter wall that was raised and reached out into the city to draw the public into its curved courtyard, which we termed the 'bubble'. Below the courtyard was a dramatic concourse, where the public could experience and participate in exhibitions, recitals, dance classes and educational programmes – or simply enjoy views over Cardiff Bay.

Conceptually, the building is a

Composite plan

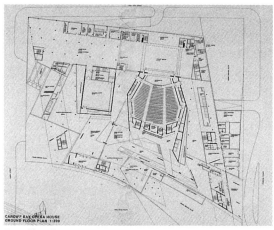

Ground-floor plan

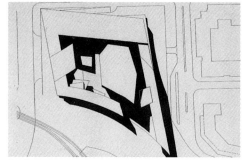

Site plan

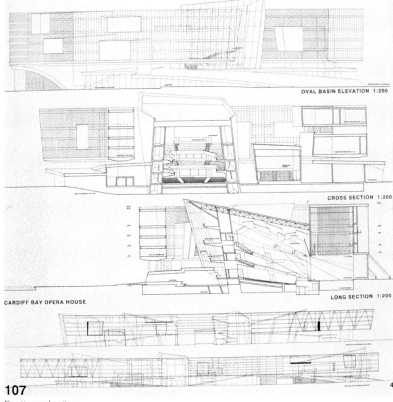

OVAL BASIN ELEVATION 1:200

CROSS SECTION 1:200

CARDIFF BAY OPERA HOUSE

LONG SECTION 1:200

107

Elevations and sections

120

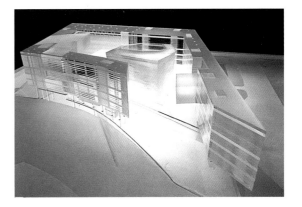

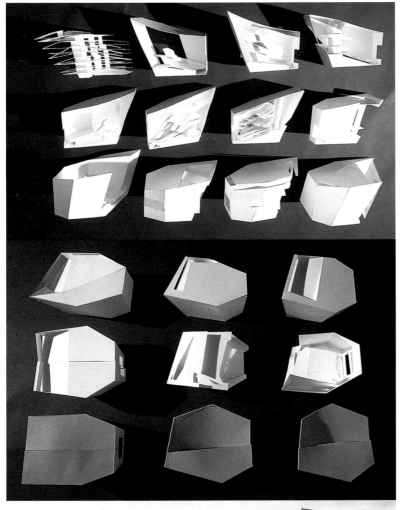

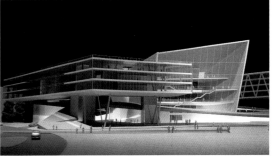

Models

Auditorium study models sequence [top and middle]; ground-condition studies [bottom]

literal opening up of the activities of an opera house. This is achieved materially through glass planes. The performance spaces, like the production and rehearsal facilities, orchestra rehearsal rooms and main auditorium, are articulated as sculptural forms and painted striking colours, which are set into the glazed wall like jewels in a necklace.

View from plaza [top]
View into interior courtyard [above]
Sectional perspective through auditorium [left]

BOILERHOUSE EXTENSION, VICTORIA AND ALBERT MUSEUM

London, 1996

The V & A is an urban block that has grown over the last 150 years, a rich patchwork of period buildings. After a process of outward expansion, the museum is looking inward, to make use of its remaining empty spaces. Our design, for the former boilerhouse, uses these voids to create accessible spaces while reflecting the V & A's role as an agent of change in architecture.

The future promises fluidity of space, an adaptive, flexible architecture made possible by lightweight modular components. Our design uses the pixel as the medium for configuration, whether on the scale of a display panel, an exhibition cabinet or a space.

The first architectural move is to raise the main building so that Exhibition Road can be directly connected to the Pirelli Gardens, allowing the ground-floor wing to be opened up to incorporate a restaurant fronting the garden. This large public area penetrates deep

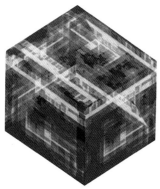

Pixelation

124

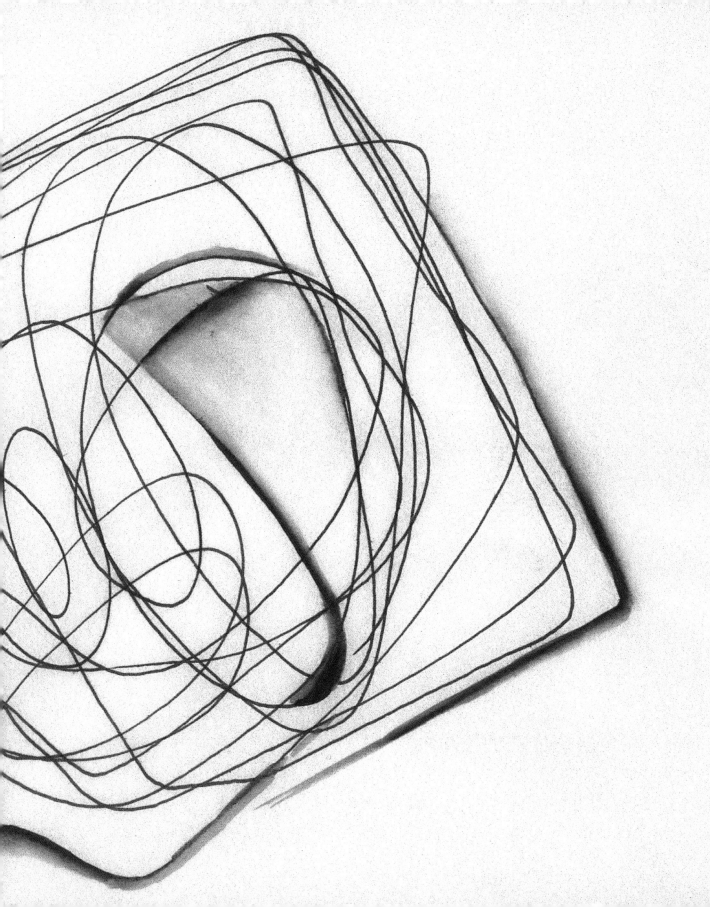

into the existing museum and creates shops, gardens and a series of entrances in the gallery wings.

The top three floors are interlocking volumes that house the educational and events centre, administration and plant rooms and connect to the museum's existing wings. Between these solids, voids are cut into the roof and elevations to bring in daylight and inserted into the areas between the existing façades and the new building so that Aston Webb's elevations can still be seen.

The façade is made of two skins that serve specific functions but that weave and sometimes merge with each other to form floors, walls and windows. The outer skin is a rain-screen made of standard-size flat panels in glass and metal and makes use of an overlap detail to create an undulating surface. The inner skin incorporates blinds for solar protection and for blackouts for exhibitions.

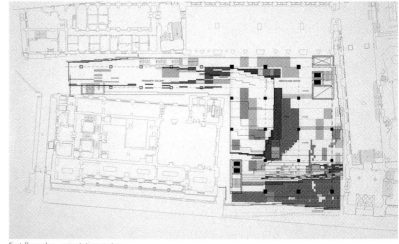

First-floor plan – orientation centre

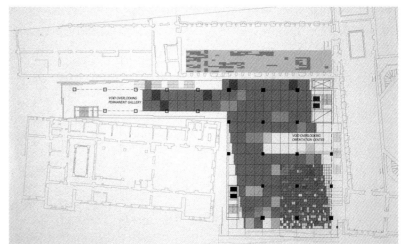

Second-floor plan – temporary exhibition hall

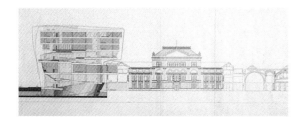

Long section

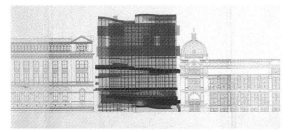

Front elevation

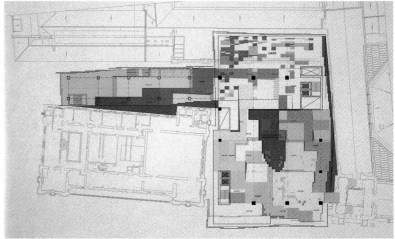

Third- /fourth-floor plans – permanent galleries

126

View from entrance [above]
Sectional perspective [left]

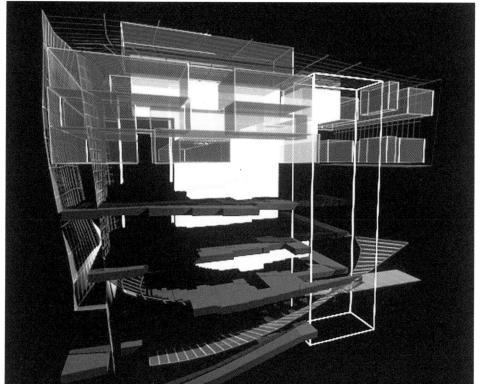

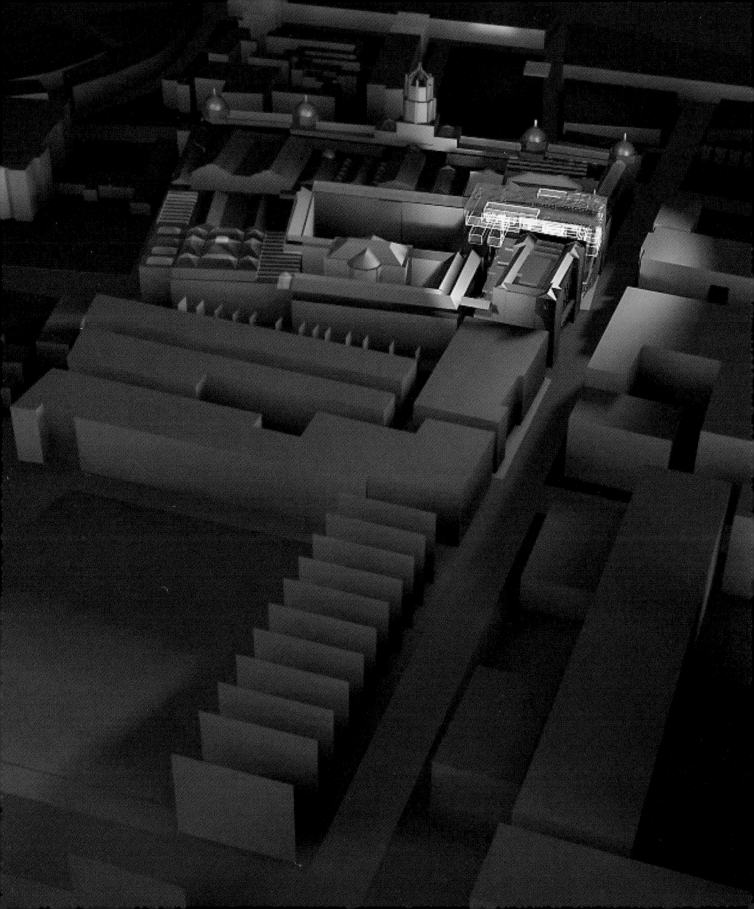

Aerial view [left]
Sectional perspective [below]
Roofscape [bottom]
Street-level view [right]
Aerial perspective [below right]

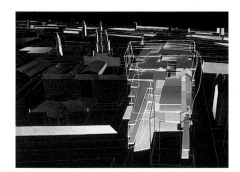

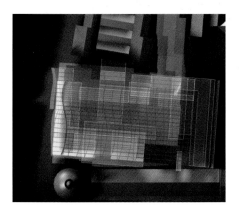

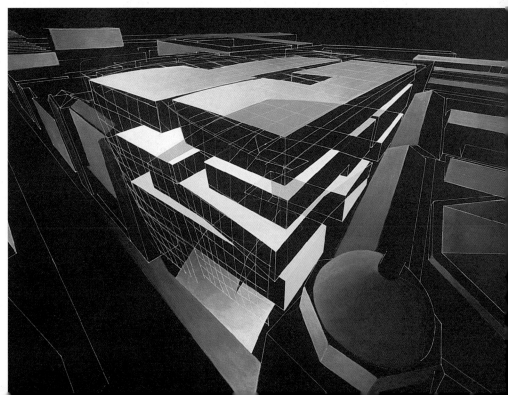

WISH MACHINE:
WORLD INVENTION

Kunsthalle, Vienna, 1996

In collaboration with Patrik Schumacher

The architectural interpretation of humanity's tangle of fact and fiction cannot be reduced to ideal, Platonic forms. Nothing is conceived a priori. The exhibition spaces are thus ambiguous perspectival effects of a bundle of walls. The walls emerge at the point of entry and traverse the box – which can barely contain them – in all directions. Without a prescribed route, surprises are inevitable.

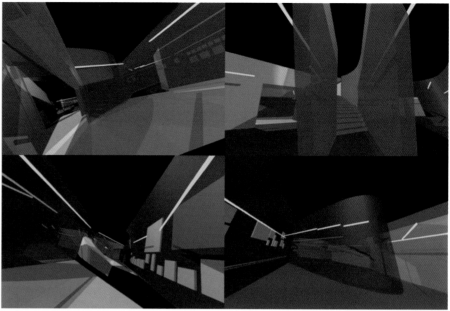

Interior perspectives

Exploded isometric

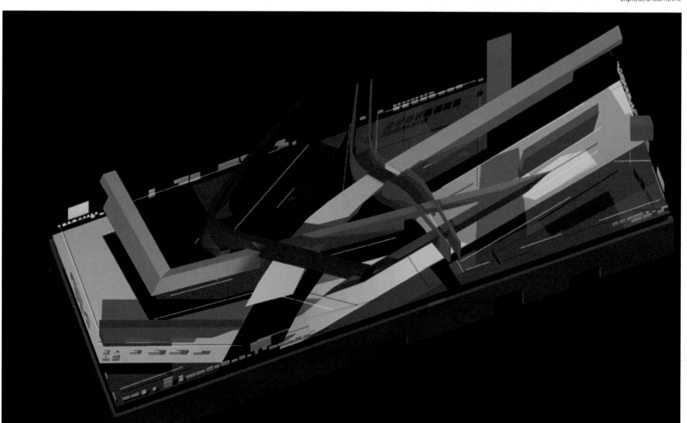

PAPER ART

Leopold-Hoesch Museum, Düren,
Germany, 1996

The exhibition space was marked by
an ordered 'wholeness' that
somehow seemed to have rendered
the space static. To counter this
immobility, we attempted to
materialize more dynamic qualities,
such as speed, intensity, power and
direction. The openings – doorways,
corridors – into the entrance hall
serve as witnesses to an event, the
act of capturing an infinite number
of temporary images witnessed by
the viewers' changing perspectives.
These successive images combine
to form a space born of motion, a
new image of architectural presence.

The material interplay between
the paper, transient by nature, and
the solidity of the existing space is
important: the paper's lightness
and movement capture the
spontaneousness and ephemerality
that the invisible traces of motion
manifest.

MASTER'S SECTION

Venice Biennale, Palazzo Grassi,
Venice, 1996

The space was an elliptical room and
a small adjacent terrace. Because all
four sides of the room were
connected to the major circulation
routes, we emphasized the space's
volume but did not interfere with
visitor traffic by emancipating the
wall display space from the floor and
suspending it two metres high. The
manner in which paintings,
drawings, models and reliefs were
composed on the walls created a
'super-image'.

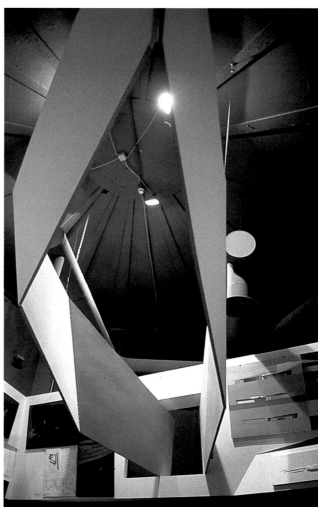

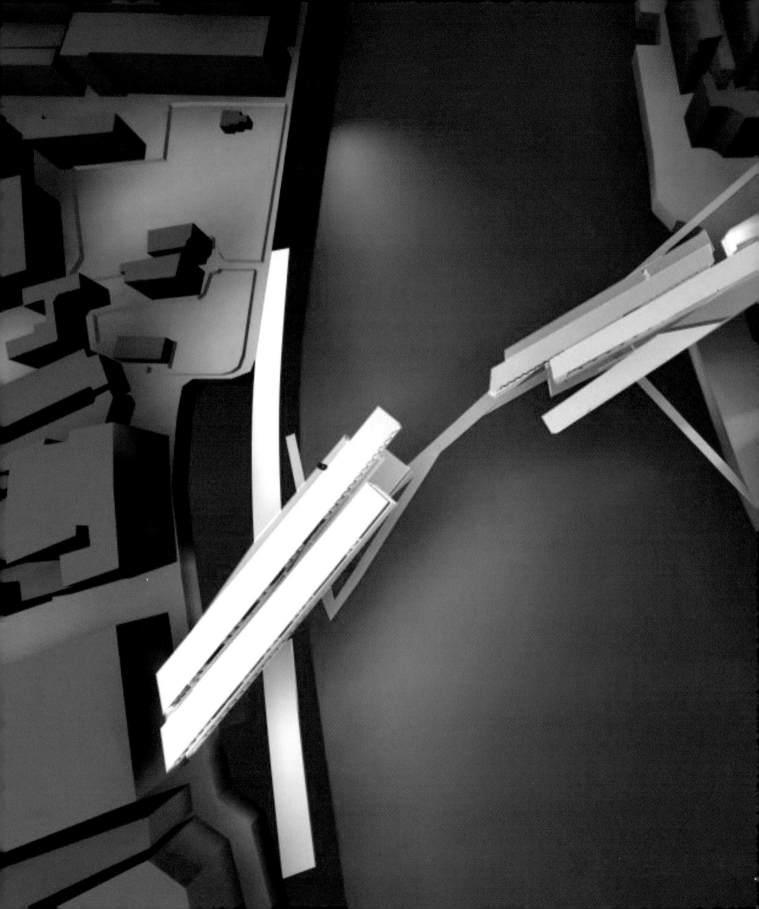

HABITABLE BRIDGE

London, 1996

Aerial view [left]　　　　　　　　　　　　View from north embankment [above]

With the possibility of becoming a dominant feature of the skyline, the bridge takes the form of a horizontal skyscraper that contains a variety of spaces: accommodation, retail, cultural and recreational. Drawing on the metropolis's cultural diversity, the bridge weaves together a variety of activities and functions into a living structure.

The bridge's north side is characterized by beams that are bundled together to mirror the urban density of the riverfront. The bundle splinters apart as it reaches together, forming a series of volumes and routes that veer towards the South Bank and Coin Street. The splintering occurs at and is emphasized by an interruption – a break – in the bridge that allows views down the east–west axis, permitting a vista from Richmond in the south-west all the way to St Paul's in the east, as well as internal views of the bridge itself.

The programme is organized vertically, with free-flow public-access 'streets' – with a mixture of commercial and cultural spaces – on the lower levels and private areas – loftlike spaces that could be used as home/offices, artists' studios or workshops – in the volumes above. The spaces and routes function as a fluid whole – floor plates distort and split to create voids that maximize the river's presence.

135

Model

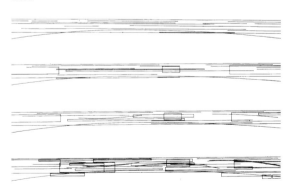

Preliminary studies

Interior perspective

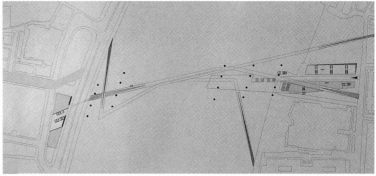
Ground-level plan

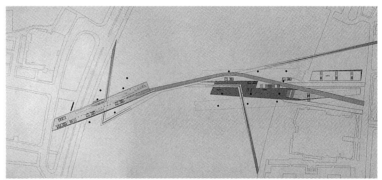
First-level plan

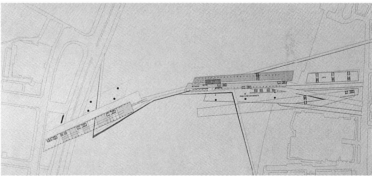
Second-level plan

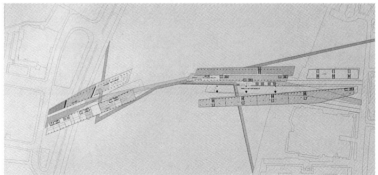
Third-level plan

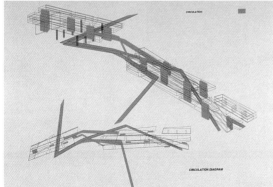
Circulation paths

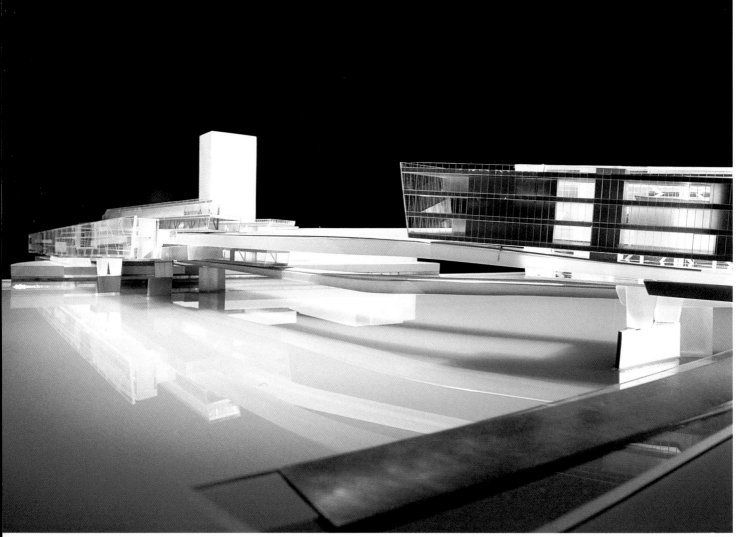

Models

Perspectives

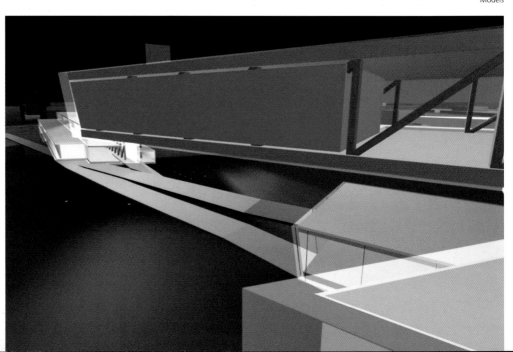

138

LA FENICE

Venice, 1996

We were commissioned by London's *Daily Telegraph* to offer a response to the fire that had devastated one of Italy's most revered opera houses, La Fenice. This theoretical work is meant to stimulate a broader discussion of rebuilding cultural and national monuments. Venice is a city of towers whose roofscape is punctuated by chimneys and spires. We wanted to contribute to this fabric with our elevated opera house. Its verticality, as rendered in period paintings and literary passages, suggested to us that its presence should be stretched and incorporated into the roofscape.

Because Venice is already a theatre in itself, we proposed to invert the plan to expose performances to the outside. We would clear the ground and create an outdoor stage and seating that faced the square and canal. We adapted the canalside to suit this staging concept, so that the canal became a stage, and the houses' façades behind it a kind of projection screen.

As in our design for the Cardiff Bay Opera House [p. 118], foyers on different levels look down from the auditorium to the square below. Goods and services arrive by canal or passage and are hoisted up the 'occupied' walls to the back and side. Similarly, the public ascend the walls to open balconies to get a better view of ground-level activities, or further up to balconies within the auditorium.

PHILHARMONIC HALL

Luxembourg, 1997

In collaboration with Patrik Schumacher

The concept that drives our scheme is 'landscape'. The steep hill facing Luxembourg's old city provided clues for exploiting the contours. We developed the idea of an artificially contoured site through a series of tiered, stepped and ramped floors, roofs and levels. Out of this landscape emerge a grand auditorium and a chamber hall.

Visitors enter the building via a gently rising ramp that leads to the lobbies at the front of house and to the auditoria's balconies and foyers, which face the view of the town. These slopes and ramps are like a continuous undulating landscape, with courtyards inserted at strategic positions to admit light to the activities at ground level.

The interiors of the auditoria extend the landscape idea, with contours that define circulation and in the rows of seating. Each auditorium has its own foyer; these face in opposite directions, with a common foyer between them.

The central difference between the two auditoria is their volumetric compositions. Both erupt from the tiered landscape as they twist and lock into place on the site. The chamber hall's glazed lobby and public gallery face a triangular balcony and act as a kind of belvedere against the grand auditorium's larger volume. In both spaces internal lines continue the contours and spiral into the halls to define stalls and balconies, as well as the finishes and features of the walls and ceilings.

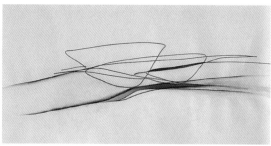

Sketches

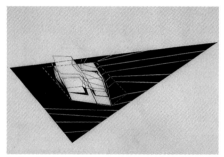
Contour drawing

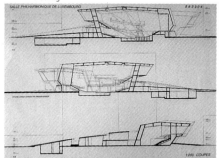
Longitudinal sections

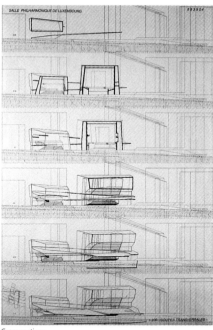
Cross sections

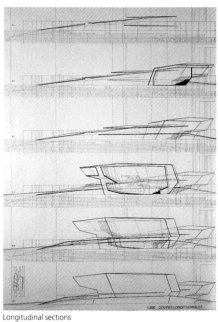
Longitudinal sections

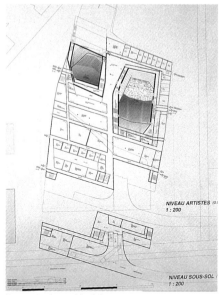
Basement and ground-level plans

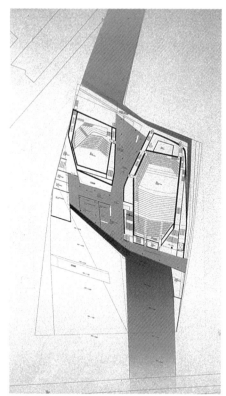
First-level plan

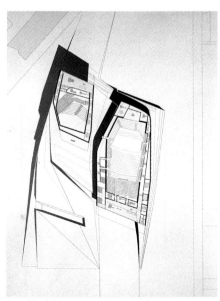
Second-level plan

146

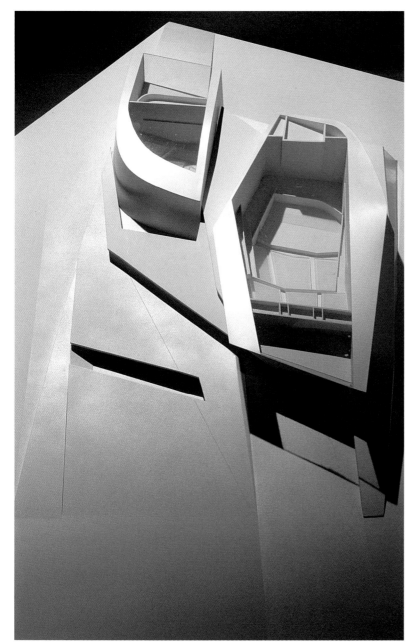

Model

Volumetric studies

Night view

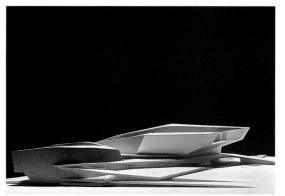

Model

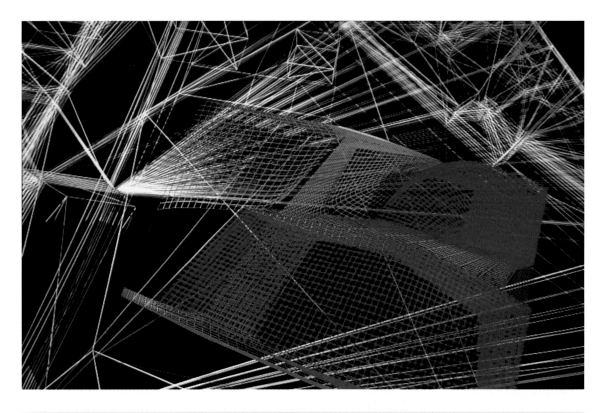

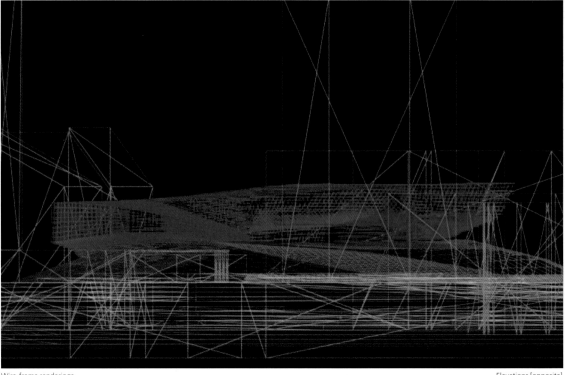

Wire-frame renderings

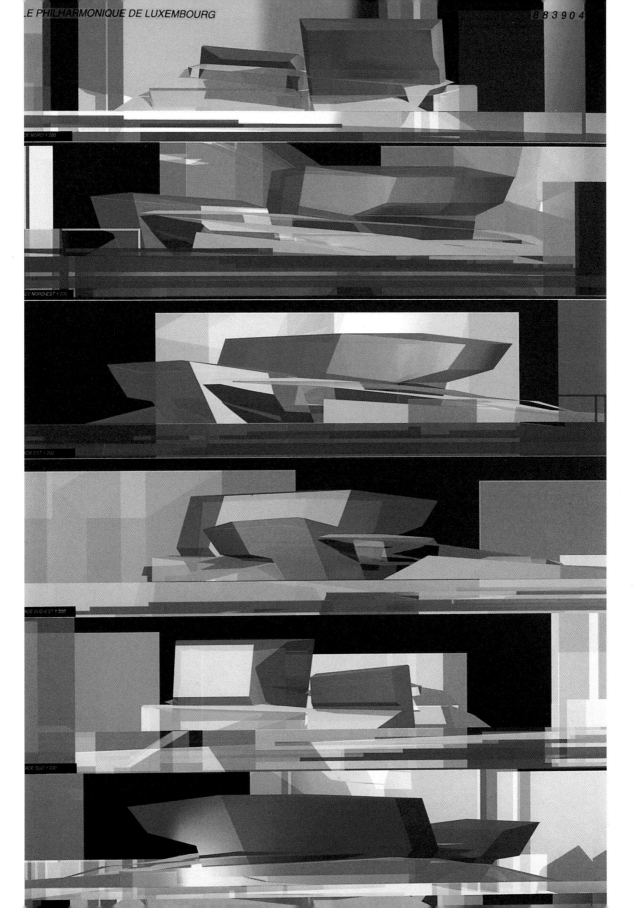

DE NORD 1:200

DE NORD-EST 1:200

DE EST 1:200

ADE SUD-EST 1:200

ADE SUD 1:200

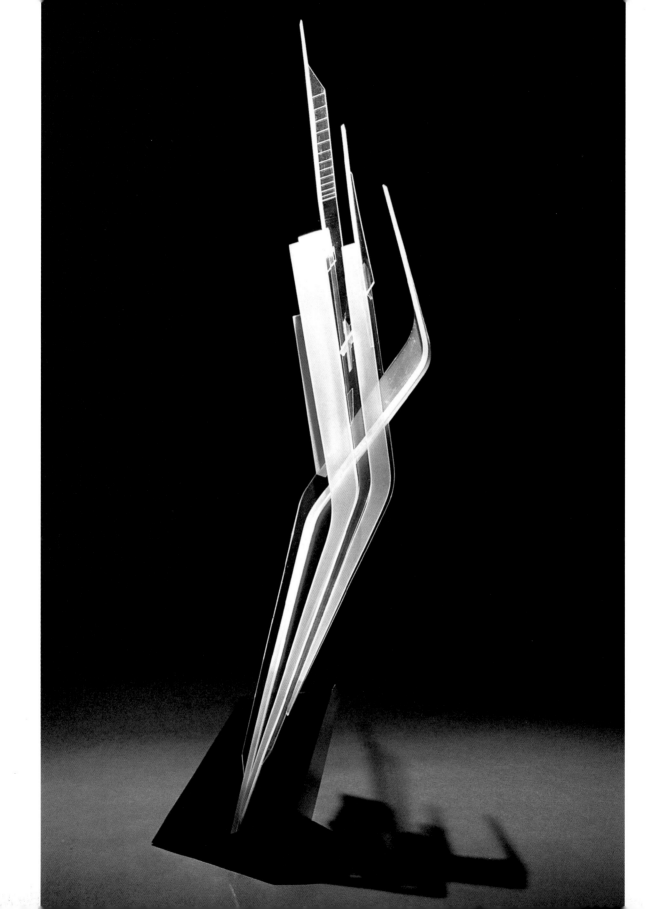

LANDESGARTENSCHAU 1999

Weil am Rhein, Germany, 1997–

In collaboration with Patrik Schumacher and Mayer Bährle

Rather than sit in the landscape as an isolated object, the exhibition hall emerges fluidly from the geometry of the surrounding network of paths, three of which entangle to form the building. Four parallel, partly interwoven spaces are caught in this bundle of paths: one snuggles up to the south side of the building, while another, gently sloping, rises over its back; the third cuts diagonally through the interior. The main spaces, exhibition hall and café stretch along these contours and permit ample sunlight and views. Secondary rooms disappear within the 'root' of the building. A terrace including a performance space is located to the south of the café.

The research centre is situated north of the exhibition hall, partly submerged into the ground in order to take advantage of the earth itself. The centre's sunken beam becomes an open mezzanine in the exhibition hall.

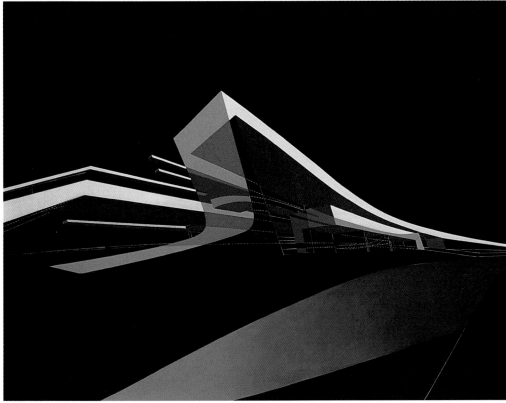

Worm's-eye view

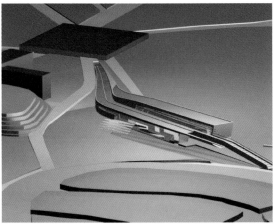

Aerial view [above]

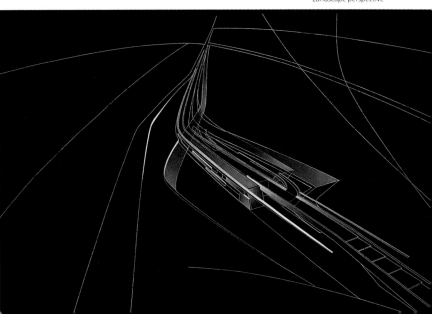

Landscape perspective

Site plan

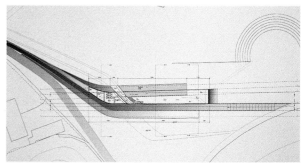

Circulation pathways

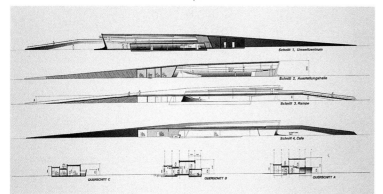

Sections

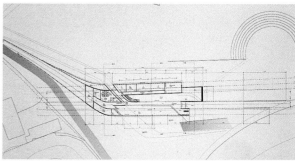

Ground-floor plan [above]   Study models [below]

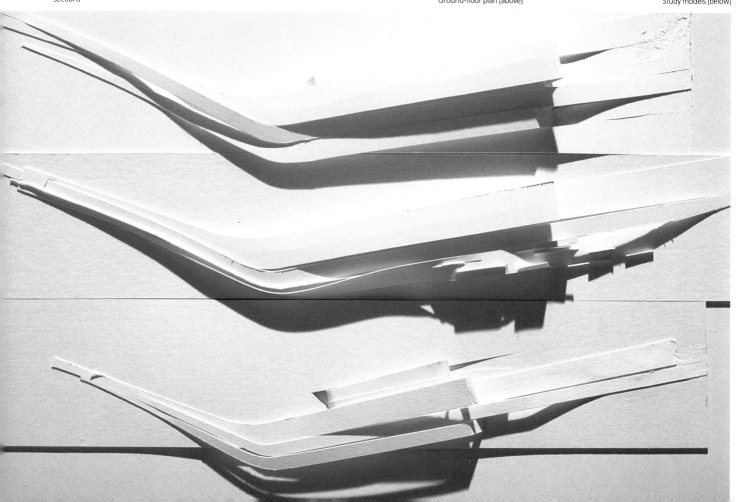

Model views [this page]
Aerial site view [following pages]

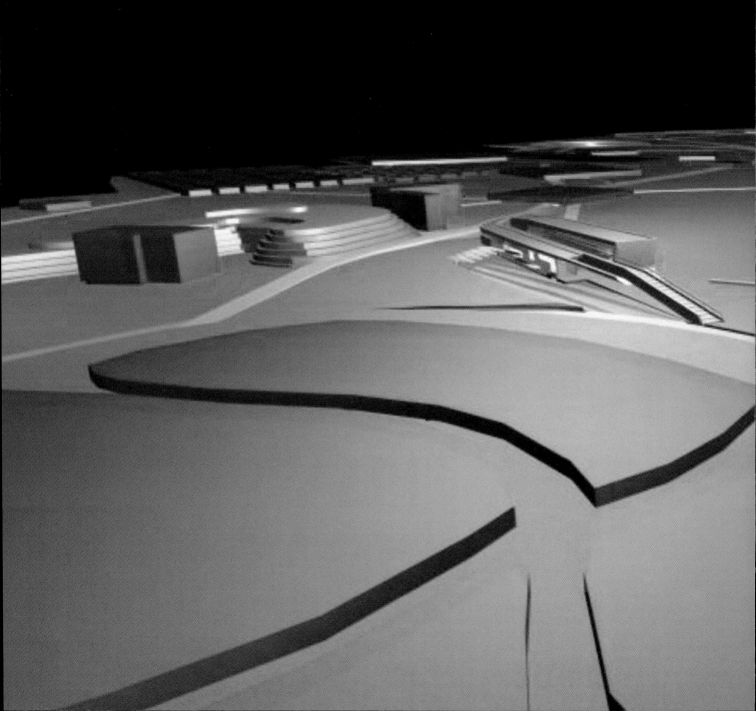

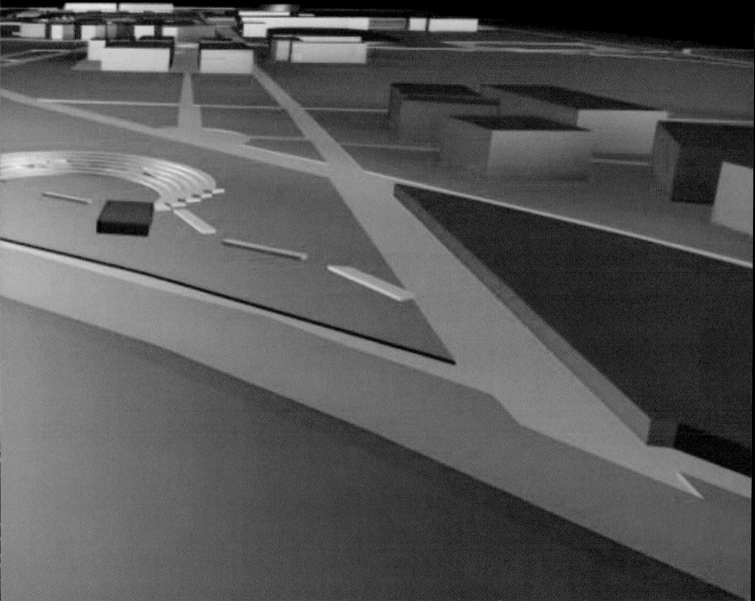

MUSEUM OF ISLAMIC ARTS

Doha, Qatar, 1997

There is no strong precedent for a nineteenth-century-style museum in the Middle East, so we developed an original typology that is rooted in the Islamic predilection for repetitive patterns punctuated by moments of difference. The building as a whole is a container for programmatic 'objects', an idea echoed in the gallery spaces: an extensive terracing of horizontal and sloped plates that house a broad spectrum of artefacts, from coins and manuscripts to glassware and carpets.

Landscape plays a vital role in the building's conception, particularly in the attempt to fuse the context with architectonic elements as seamlessly as possible. The roof is the defining feature, articulating the building as a continuous but differentiated field of spaces while mediating between the landscape, sky and galleries. Courtyards slotted into the interior provide natural light and relate to the strong tradition of courtyards, or *al-finas*, integral to Islamic architecture and planning.

The new museum is a graduated dispersal of programme which starts from the north, before descending and merging into the landscape. Administrative and educational activities cluster at the top of the site, which then curves downward into the public lobby, a landscaped tier containing the orientation lobby and announcing the collection of gallery spaces that fade towards the lower part of the site.

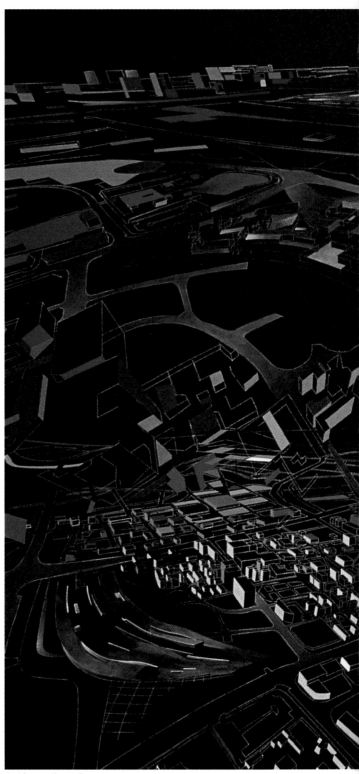

Aerial perspective rotations

Landscape-study painting

Sketches

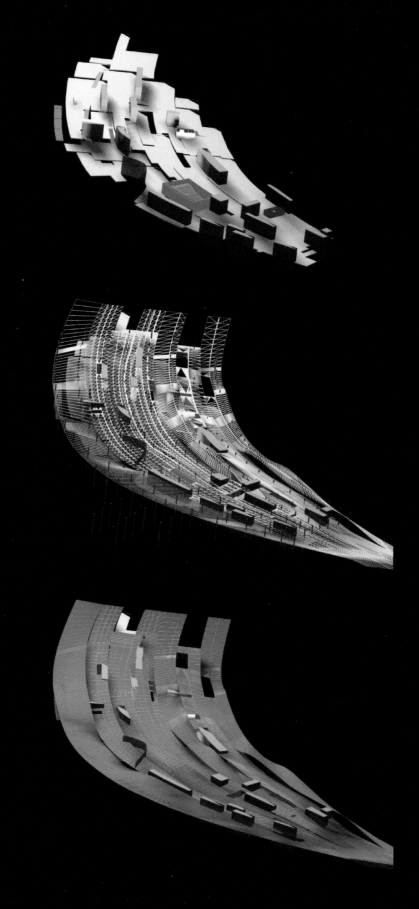

Courtyards and auditorium [p. 158, top]
Structure [p. 158, middle]
Roofscape [p. 158, bottom]
Elevations [preceding page]

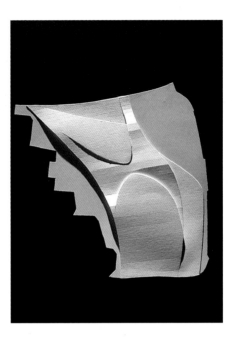

Early site studies

Interior study

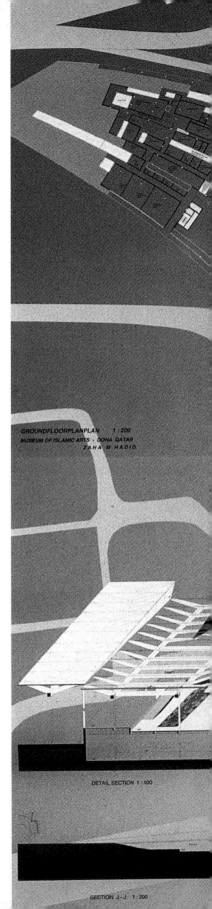

GROUNDFLOORPLANPLAN   1 : 200
MUSEUM OF ISLAMIC ARTS · DOHA QATAR
Z A H A M H A D I D

DETAIL SECTION 1 : 100

Ground plan, sections and details

SECTION J-J 1 : 200

SECTIONS   1 : 200,   1 : 500
MUSEUM OF ISLAMIC ARTS · DOHA QATAR
Z A H A   M   H A D I D

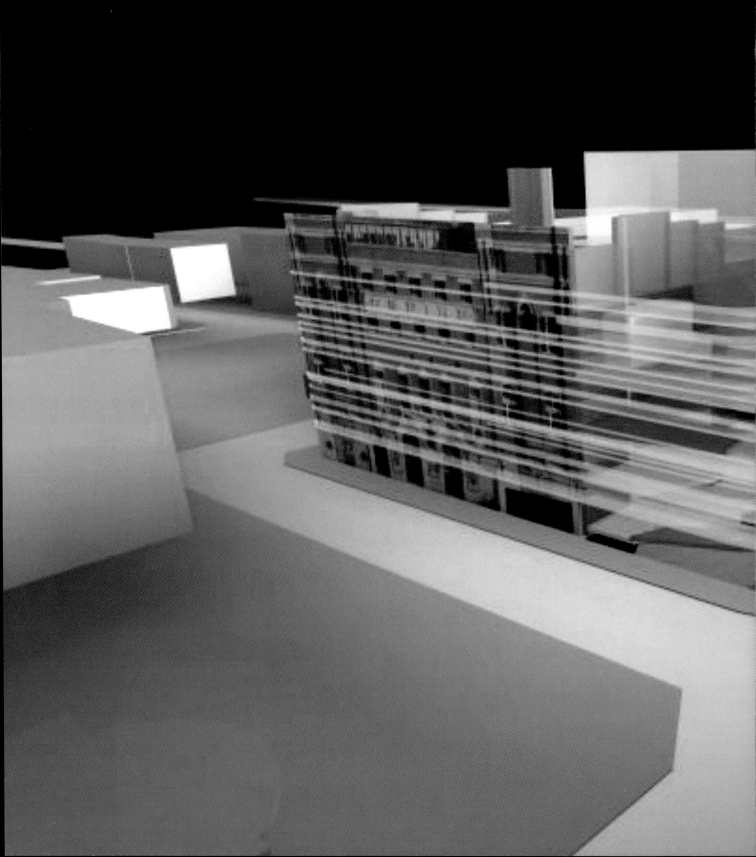

HACKNEY EMPIRE

London, 1997

A corner in north London offered the prospect of commercial development around the activities of the old Hackney Empire theatre. The central design concept is a spiral that ascends from the basement to a new fourth-floor level and cabaret theatre. We allowed the building to be essentially transparent, so that the interior would be seen as a continuously moving spiral of people and activities. Inside the existing auditorium, we opted not for a faithful historical restoration but for the use of four palettes – lighting, acoustics, texture and colour: natural and artificial lighting would be enhanced; gallery balustrades, walls, arches and ceiling would be embellished and the proscenium opening restored; seats and floor finishes would be revitalized; and an abstract expression of colour, fabric and finish would improve acoustic performance.

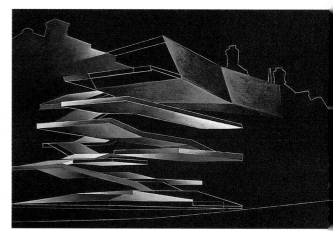

Circulation diagram

CAMPUS CENTRE

Illinois Institute of Technology,
Chicago, 1998

In collaboration with Patrik Schumacher

The proposed insertion of a student centre into Mies van der Rohe's campus offered the rich opportunity to echo the heightened awareness of difference and multiple-use patterns by social groups within the university and the texture of Chicago itself. To respond to this multiplicity and diversity, we opted for a fluid organizational system that blurred the areas of work and leisure.

The original campus master plan was based on a lateral distribution of programme. We wanted to transform this open dispersal and fold it onto itself, so that the campus's many elements came together in a compact and multilayered volume.

Approach to the building is through a play of graduating floor surfaces and curving ramps into a double-height vestibule space that orients the visitor towards the auditorium, cafeteria and retail spaces. The second floor partly peels off from the first, leaving voids that peer downward, cut by stair ramps. Meeting rooms are a matrix of sliding panels that recede and protrude according to the needs of the student associations. All of these spaces lack clearly definable edges, encouraging cross-fertilization of events; this is enhanced by a modular system of table-tops which allows for surprising configurations. The third floor culminates as a folded envelope that houses the clubrooms and the Mies Interpretive Center.

Preliminary sketch

Study plan

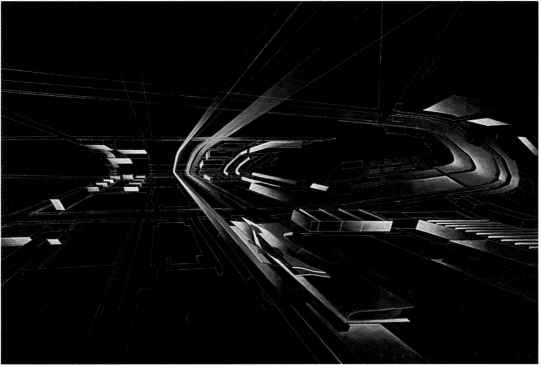

Folding campus onto itself

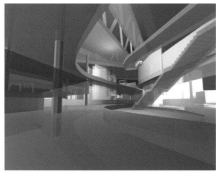

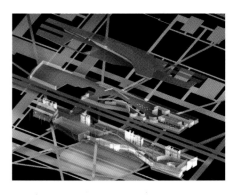

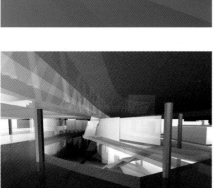
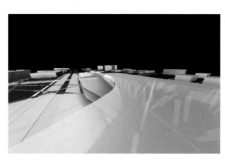
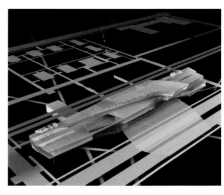

Computer renderings of
interior, perspective, exploded
and aerial views [above]

First-floor plan [right]
Ground-floor study [far right]
Second-floor plan [below right]
Second-floor field study
[below far right]

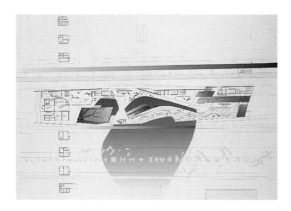
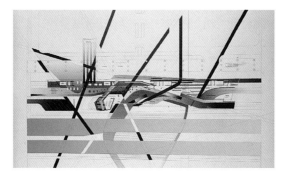
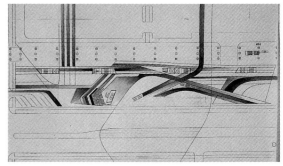
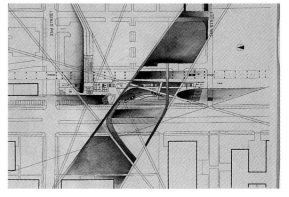

166

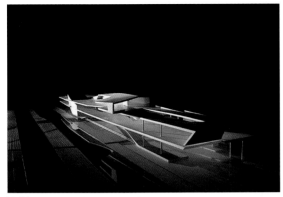 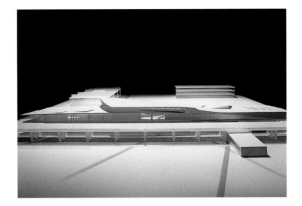

Models

Composite of study models

CONTEMPORARY ARTS CENTRE

Cincinnati, 1998–

One of the most exciting aspects of the brief for this new contemporary art museum was that it would not be built around a permanent collection. Rather, it would be a container for temporary exhibitions showing a wide variety of work, which in turn would allow an exciting degree of unpredictability between a given show and the architecture.

The building consists of four main features. An 'urban carpet' was conceived to create a simultaneously horizontal and vertical composition – as if the city's grid had been curved upward – to maximize the space's potential as a public lobby while mediating between the city and galleries. The second aspect is that of anti-gravity – recalling Magritte's suspended rock. This is the tension that is created between gallery spaces that appear to be carved from a single block and their lightness as they hover over the lobby. The exhibition spaces themselves are linked together in a kind of three-dimensional jigsaw puzzle, the design's third characteristic. Finally, the building's exterior presents an animated skin, a collage of transparent elements that weave into the galleries' mass and reveal a texture of activity and art in constant flux, thus enlivening the building as a whole.

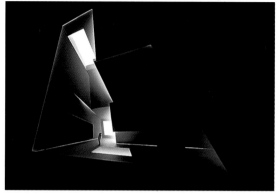

Light study of second-floor gallery space [above and below]

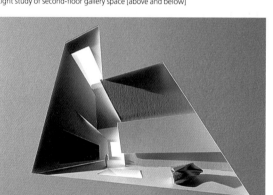

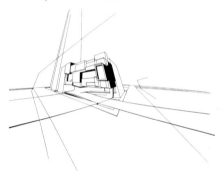

View from plaza on Walnut Street

View from West Sixth Street and Walnut Street

Unfolded site study [above]

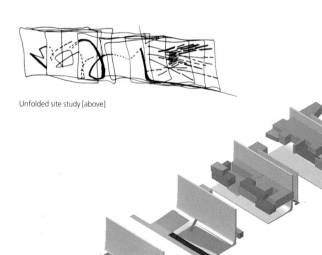

Isometric program distribution [above]
Model of urban carpet and vertical circulation system [right]

FURNITURE AND OBJECTS

Red sofa (1988)

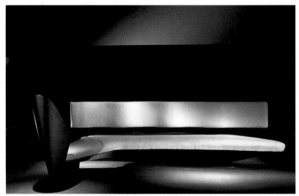

Wave sofa (1988)

Whoosh sofa (1988)

Warped Plane Lamp (1987)

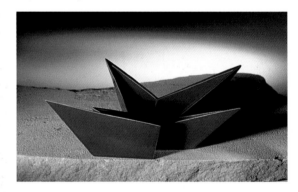

Waecthenberg ceramics

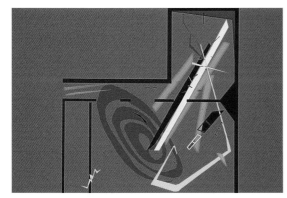

Vorwerk wall-to-wall carpeting (1990)

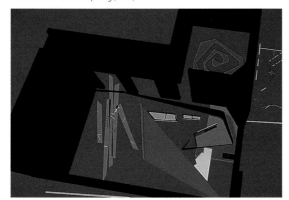

Vorwerk wall-to-wall carpeting (1990)

Vorwerk wall-to-wall carpeting (1990)

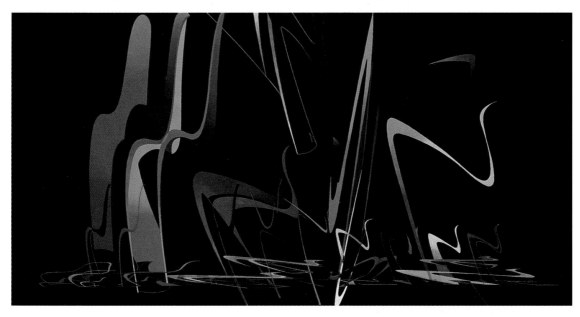

Hommage à Verner Panton, Vitra (1990)

PROJECT INFORMATION

MALEVICH'S TEKTONIK
London, 1976–77
Fourth-year Student Project

MUSEUM OF THE NINETEENTH CENTURY
London, 1977–78
Fifth-year Student Design Thesis

DUTCH PARLIAMENT EXTENSION
The Hague, 1978–79
DESIGN TEAM Office for Metropolitan Architecture (OMA): Zaha Hadid, Rem Koolhaas, Elia Zenghelis, with Richard Perlmutter, Ron Steiner, E. Veneris

IRISH PRIME MINISTER'S RESIDENCE
Dublin, 1979–80
DESIGN TEAM Zaha Hadid with K. Ahari, Jonathan Dunn

59 EATON PLACE
London, 1981–82
Residential Conversion
DESIGN TEAM Zaha Hadid with Jonathan Dunn, K. Knapkiewicz, Bijan Ganjei, Wendy Galway

PARC DE LA VILLETTE
Science Park Masterplan
Paris, 1982–83
DESIGN TEAM Zaha Hadid with Jonathan Dunn, Marianne van der Waals, Michael Wolfson

THE PEAK
Hong Kong, 1982–83
Leisure Club, International Competition: First Prize
DESIGN TEAM Zaha Hadid with Michael Wolfson, Jonathan Dunn, Marianne van der Waals, N. Ayoubi
PRESENTATION Michael Wolfson, Alistair Standing, Nan Lee, Wendy Galway
STRUCTURAL ENGINEER Ove Arup and Partners – David Thomlinson

THE WORLD (89 DEGREES)
1983
Painting

GRAND BUILDINGS
London, 1985
Mixed-use Development for Trafalgar Square
DESIGN TEAM Zaha Hadid with (in the early stages) Brian Ma Siy
COMPETITION TEAM Michael Wolfson, Brian Ma Siy, Marianne Palme, Kar-Hwa Ho, Piers Smerin

HALKIN PLACE
Residential Conversion
London, 1985
DESIGN TEAM Zaha Hadid with Brian Ma Siy, Piers Smerin

MELBURY COURT
London, 1985
Residential Conversion
DESIGN TEAM Zaha Hadid with Brian Ma Siy, Michael Wolfson

TENTS AND CURTAINS
Milan Triennale, 1985
DESIGN Zaha Hadid with Piers Smerin, Michael Wolfson

KYOTO INSTALLATIONS
Kyoto, 1985
Installations

24 CATHCART ROAD
London, 1985–86
Residential Interior and Furniture
CLIENT William Bitar, London
DESIGN TEAM Zaha Hadid with Michael Wolfson, Brett Steele, Nan Lee, Brenda MacKneson
TOTAL FLOOR AREA 435 m² (1 floor)

HAMBURG DOCKLANDS
Hamburg, 1986
Masterplanning Workshops

NEW YORK, MANHATTAN
1986
Painting

KURFÜRSTENDAMM 70
Berlin, 1986
Office Building
CLIENT Euwo Holdings AG, Berlin
DESIGN TEAM Zaha Hadid with Michael Wolfson, Brett Steele, Piers Smerin, Charles Crawford, Nicola Cousins, David Gomersall
TOTAL FLOOR AREA 820 m² (7 floors)
CLIENT FEASABILITY Berlin Senate
CO-ARCHITECT Stefan Schroth, Berlin
STRUCTURAL ENGINEER Ove Arup and Partners with Peter Rice, John Thornton
GLAZING CONSULANT RFR, Paris – Hugh Dutton
QUANTITY SURVEYOR Büro AM Lutzowplatz with Wilfraed Kralt

IBA HOUSING
Berlin, 1986–93
Internationale Bau-Ausstellung
CLIENT DEGEWO, Berlin
DESIGN TEAM Zaha Hadid with Michael Wolfson, David Gomersall, Piers Smerin, David Winslow, Paivi Jaaskelainen
TOTAL FLOOR AREA 2500 m² (long block: 3 floors; tower: 8 floors)
CO-ARCHITECT Stefan Schroth, Berlin

AZABU-JYUBAN
Tokyo, 1986
Commercial Development
CLIENT K-One Corporation, Tokyo
DESIGN TEAM Zaha Hadid with Michael Wolfson, Brenda MacKneson, Alistair Standing, Signy Svalastoga, Paul Brislin, Nicola Cousins, David Gomersall, Edgar Gonzalez, Erik Hemmingway, Simon Koumjian, Paivi Jaaskelainen
MODEL Daniel Chadwick, Tim Price
TOTAL FLOOR AREA 340 m² (6 floors)
PROJECT ARCHITECT IN JAPAN Satoshi Ohashi

CO-ARCHITECT Hisashi Kobayashi & Associates
STRUCTURAL ENGINEER Ove Arup and Partners with Peter Rice, Yasuo Tamura

TOMIGAYA
Tokyo, 1986
Office Building
CLIENT K-One Corporation, Tokyo
DESIGN TEAM Zaha Hadid with Michael Wolfson, Brenda MacKneson, Alistair Standing, Signy Svalastoga, Paul Brislin, Nicola Cousins, David Gomersall, Edgar Gonzalez, Erik Hemmingway, Simon Koumjian, Paivi Jaaskelainen, Patrik Schumacher
MODEL Daniel Chadwick, Tim Price
TOTAL FLOOR AREA 238 m² (2 floors)
PROJECT ARCHITECT IN JAPAN Satoshi Ohashi
CO-ARCHITECT Hisashi Kobayashi & Associates
STRUCTURAL ENGINEER Ove Arup and Partners with Peter Rice, Yasuo Tamura

WEST HOLLYWOOD CIVIC CENTRE
Los Angeles, 1987

AL WAHDA SPORTS CENTRE
Abu Dhabi, 1988
CLIENT Sheikh Tahnoon bin Saeed Al Nayiyan
DESIGN TEAM Zaha Hadid with Michael Wolfson, Satoshi Ohashi
STRUCTURAL ENGINEER Ove Arup and Partners with Peter Rice

METROPOLIS
Institute of Contemporary Arts, London, 1988
Installation

BERLIN 2000
1988
Painting

VICTORIA CITY AREAL
Berlin, 1988
Mixed-use Development (Retail, Offices, Hotel)
CLIENT City of Berlin (Building Authority)
DESIGN TEAM Zaha Hadid with Michael Wolfson, Nicholas Boyarsky, Patrik Schumacher, Edgar Gonzalez, Paul Brislin, Nicola Cousins, Signy Svalastoga, C. J. Lim, Kim Lee Chai, Israel Numes, Mathew Wells, Simon Koumjian
MODEL Daniel Chadwick
TOTAL FLOOR AREA approx. 75,000 m² (15 floors)
STRUCTURAL ENGINEER Ove Arup and Partners with Peter Rice, Mathew Wells

A NEW BARCELONA
1989
Urban Masterplan
DESIGN TEAM Zaha Hadid with Patrik Schumacher, Simon Koumjian, Edgar Gonzalez

TOKYO FORUM
Tokyo, 1989
Cultural Centre
DESIGN TEAM Zaha Hadid with Brian Ma Siy, Patrik Schumacher, Vincent Marol, Philippa Makin, Brian Langlands, David Gomersall, Jonathan Nsubuga
MODEL Daniel Chadwick
TOTAL FLOOR AREA 135,000 m² (8 floors)

HAFENSTRASSE DEVELOPMENT
Hamburg, 1989
Mixed-use Development (Housing, Office, Retail)
CLIENT The Free Hansestadt Hamburg (Building Authority)
DESIGN TEAM Zaha Hadid, Patrik Schumacher, Signy Svalastoga, Edgar Gonzalez, Brain Langlands, Philippa Makin, Nicola Cousins, Mario Gooden, Ursula Gonsior, Claudia Busch, Vincent Marol
MODEL Daniel Chadwick
TOTAL FLOOR AREA corner building: 871 m² (8 floors); middle site building: approx. 2800 m² (10 floors)
CO-ARCHITECT Mirjane Markovic, Hamburg
STRUCTURAL ENGINEER Ove Arup and Partners with Peter Rice

MOONSOON
Sapporo, Japan, 1989–90
Restaurant
CLIENT Jasmac Corporation, Japan
DESIGN TEAM Zaha Hadid with Bill Goodwin, Shin Egashira, Kar Hwa Ho, Edgar Gonzalez, Brian Langlands, Ed Gaskin, Yuko Moriyama, Urit Luden, Craig Kiner, Dianne Hunter-Gorman, Patrik Schumacher
MODEL Daniel Chadwick
CONSULTANTS Michael Wolfson, Satoshi Ohashi, David Gomersall
TOTAL FLOOR AREA 435 m² (2 floors)
PRODUCER Axe Co, Ltd, Japan

FOLLY 3
Osaka, 1989–90
International Garden Festival
ORGANIZER Workshop for Architecture & Urbanism, Tokyo
GENERAL PRODUCER Arata Isozaki
CLIENT AND SPONSOR Fukuoka Jisho Co Ltd, Fukuoka, Japan
DESIGN TEAM Zaha Hadid, Edgar Gonzalez, Urit Luden, Satoshi Ohashi, Kar Hwa Ho, Patrik Schumacher, Voon Yee-Wong, Simon Koumjian, Dianne Hunter-Gorman, Nicola Cousins, David Gomersall
MODEL Daniel Chadwick
TOTAL FLOOR AREA 435 m²
CONTRACTOR Zenitaka Corporation

LEICESTER SQUARE
London, 1990
CLIENT *Blueprint* Magazine, London
DESIGN TEAM Zaha Hadid with Graham Modlen and Vincent Marol, Simon Koumjian, Patrik Schumacher, Craig Kiner, Cristina Verissimo, David Gomersall, Philippa Makin, Dianne Hunter-Gorman, Maria Rossi, Mya Manakides

VITRA FIRE STATION
Weil am Rhein, Germany, 1990–94
CLIENT Rolf Fehlbaum, Dr. Phil., Vitra International AG, Basel, Switzerland
DESIGN Zaha Hadid
PROJECT ARCHITECT Patrik Schumacher
DETAIL DESIGN Patrik Schumacher, Signy Svalastoga
DESIGN TEAM Simon Koumjian, Edgar Gonzalez, Kar Wha Ho, Voon Yee-Wong, Craig Kiner, Cristina Verissimo, Maria Rossi,

Daniel R. Oakley, Nicola Cousins, David Gomersall, Olaf Weishaupt

MODELS Daniel Chadwick, Tim Price

PROJECT MANAGEMENT, CONSTRUCTION

DRAWINGS AND BUILDING SUPERVISION GPF & Assoziierte, Roland Mayer with Jürgen Roth, Shahriar Eetezadi, Eva Weber, Wolfgang Mehnert

ART AND MEDIA CENTRE
Düsseldorf, 1989–93

CLIENT Kunst- und Medienzentrum Rheinhafen GmbH

DESIGN Zaha Hadid

PROJECT ARCHITECTS Brett Steele and Brian Ma Siy

PROJECT TEAM Paul Brislin, Cathleen Chua, John Comparelli, Elden Croy, Craig Kiner, Graeme Little, Yousif Albustani, Daniel R. Oakley, Patrik Schumacher, Alistair Standing, Tuta Barbosa, David Gomersall, C. J. Lim

FEASIBILITY AND COMPETITION Michael Wolfson, Anthony Owen, Signy Svalastoga, Edgar Gonzalez, Craig Kiner, Patrik Schumacher, Ursula Gonsior, Bryan Langlands, Ed Gaskin, Yuko Moriyama, Graeme Little, Cristina Verissimo, Maria Rossi, Yousif Albustani

CONSULTANT ARCHITECT Roland Mayer, Lörrach, Germany

PROJECT MANAGER Vebau GmbH

PROJECT CO-ORDINATOR Weidleplan Consulting GmbH

MODELS Ademir Volic, Daniel Chadwick

STRUCTURAL ENGINEERS Boll und Partner, Ove Arup and Partners

SERVICES ENGINEERS Jaeger, Mornhinweg und Partner, Ove Arup and Partners, Ingenieurbüro für Elektrotechnik Werner Schwarz GmbH

COST CONSULTANT Tillyard GmbH

FAÇADE CONSULTANT Institut für Facadentechnik

FIRE SPECIALIST Wilfred Teschke

BUILDING PHYSICIST Schäcke & Bayer GmbH

TRAFFIC CONSULTANT Waning Consult GmbH

MUSIC VIDEO PAVILION
Groningen, The Netherlands, 1990

CLIENT City Planning Dept. Groningen & Museum

DESIGN TEAM Zaha Hadid with Graham Modlen, Urit Luden, Edgar Gonzalez, Vincent Marol, Maria Rossi, Dianne Hunter-Gorman, Cristina Verissimo, Yousif Albustani, Craig Moffatt, Craig Kiner

MODEL Daniel Chadwick

TOTAL FLOOR AREA 24.5 m² (4 levels: ground, 2 balconies and video room)

CO-ARCHITECT Karelse Van der Meer, Groningen

HOTEL AND RESIDENTIAL COMPLEX
Abu Dhabi, 1990

CLIENT Sheikh Tahnoon bin Saeed Al Nayiyan

DESIGN TEAM Zaha Hadid, Vincent Marol, Craig Kiner, Yousif Albustani, Satoshi Ohashi, Patrik Schumacher, Daniel R. Oakley, Philippa Makin, Dianne Hunter-Gorman

MODEL Daniel Chadwick

TOTAL FLOOR AREA 47,000 m² (2 retail floors, 1 office floor, 28 hotel floors)

STRUCTURAL ENGINEER Ove Arup and Partners

INTERZUM 91
Gluzendorf, Germany, 1990
Exhibition Stand Design

LONDON 2066
London, 1991
Painting

CLIENT *Vogue* Magazine (U.K.)

DESIGN TEAM Zaha Hadid with Daniel R. Oakley, Voon Yee-Wong, Graham Modlen, Craig Kiner, Cristina Verissimo, Yousif Albustani, Patrik Schumacher, Mascha Kosmatschof, Graeme Little

COMPUTER MODELLING Daniel R. Oakley

THE HAGUE VILLAS
The Hague, 1991
Residential

DESIGN TEAM Zaha Hadid with Craig Kiner, Patrik Schumacher, Yousif Albustani, James Braam, Daniel R. Oakley, John Stewart, Cristina Verissimo, David Gomersall

MODELS Craig Kiner

STRUCTURAL ENGINEER Ove Arup and Partners

THE GREAT UTOPIA
Solomon R. Guggenheim Museum, New York, 1992
Exhibition Design

DESIGN TEAM Zaha Hadid with Patrik Schumacher, Yousif Albustani, Daniel R. Oakley, David Gomersall, Simon Koumjian

MODELS Tim Price, Ademir Volic

VISION FOR MADRID
1992
Urban Masterplan

DESIGN TEAM Zaha Hadid with Patrik Schumacher, Daniel R. Oakley, Simon Koumjian, Yousif Albustani, Craig Kiner, Paco Mejias

BILLIE STRAUSS ART HOTEL
Nabern, Germany, 1992

DESIGN TEAM Zaha Hadid with Patrik Schumacher, Yousif Albustani, Daniel R. Oakley, David Gomersall

CONCERT HALL
Copenhagen, 1992–93

DESIGN Zaha Hadid with Patrik Schumacher

DESIGN TEAM Paul Brislin, Brian Ma Siy, John Comparelli, Nicola Cousins, Edgar Gonzalez, Douglas Grieco, C.J. Lim, Mya Manakides, Guido Schwark

STRUCTURAL ENGINEER Ove Arup and Partners

ACOUSTIC ENGINEER Arup Acoustics – Malcolm Wright

THEATRE CONSULTANT Theatre Projects Consultant

RHEINAUHAFEN REDEVELOPMENT
Cologne, 1992
Urban Masterplan

DESIGN Zaha Hadid

DESIGN TEAM Patrik Schumacher, Daniel R. Oakley, Craig Kiner, Yousif Albustani, Cathleen Chua, David Gomersall, John Stuart, Simon Koumjian

MODEL Tim Price

CARNUNTUM
Vienna, 1993
Archaeological Museum, Belvedere, Amphitheatre, Folly, Pavilion

DESIGN TEAM Zaha Hadid and Patrik Schumacher with Douglas Grieco, Wendy Ing, Brian Ma Siy, Paola Sanguinetti, Edgar Gonzalez, David Gomersall

MODEL Dan Chadwick

SPITTELAU VIADUCTS
Vienna, 1994–
Mixed-use Development (Housing, Retail, Offices)

CLIENT SEG Developers, Vienna

DESIGN Zaha Hadid with Edgar Gonzalez, Douglas Grieco, Paul Brislin, Patrik Schumacher, Woody K.T. Yao

PROJECT ARCHITECTS Woody K.T. Yao and Markus Dochantschi

DETAIL DESIGN Zaha Hadid with Woody K.T. Yao, Markus Dochantschi, Wassim Halabi, Garin O'Aivazian, James Geiger

DESIGN TEAM Clarissa Mathews, Paola Sanguinetti, Peter Ho, Anne Save de Beaurecueil, David Gomersall

TOTAL FLOOR AREA 2,600 m²

STRUCTURAL ENGINEER Dipl. Ing. Friedreich & Partner, Vienna

SPITTALMARKT
Berlin, 1995
Corporate Headquarters for German Building Society

PROJECT PARTNER Patrik Schumacher

COMPETITION TEAM Zaha Hadid, Patrik Schumacher, Woody K.T. Yao, Wassim Halabi, David Gomersall, Graham Modlen

DESIGN DEVELOPMENT Patrik Schumacher, James Geiger

LYCEE FRANÇAIS CHARLES DE GAULLE
London, 1995
Schoolhouse Extension

DESIGN TEAM Zaha Hadid with Douglas Grieco, Edgar Gonzalez, Paul Brislin, Brian Ma Siy, Paola Sanguinetti, Woody K.T. Yao, David Gomersall

PANCRAS LANE
London, 1996
Office Building over Public Space

DESIGN TEAM Zaha Hadid with Brian Ma Siy, Paul Brislin, Edgar Gonzalez, Patrik Schumacher, Douglas Grieco, Woody K.T. Yao, Paola Sanguinetti

42ND STREET HOTEL
New York, 1995
Hotels and Commercial Complex

CLIENTS Weiler Amow Management Co, Milstein Properties

DESIGN TEAM Zaha Hadid, Douglas Grieco, Peter Ho, Clarissa Matthews, Anne Save de Beaurecueil, Voon Yee-Wong, Woody K.T. Yao, Paul Brislin, Graham Modlen, Patrik Schumacher, David Gomersall, Bijan Ganjei

MODEL Richard Arminger

IMAGES FOR MODEL Dick Stracker

COMPUTER IMAGERY Rolando Kraeher

TOTAL FLOOR AREA 180,000 m²

STRUCTURAL ENGINEER Ove Arup and Partners

BLUEPRINT PAVILION
National Exhibition Centre, Birmingham, England, 1995
Exhibition Stand

CLIENT *Blueprint* Magazine, Montgomery Exhibitions Ltd.

DESIGN Zaha Hadid with Paul Brislin, Woody K.T. Yao

DESIGN TEAM Tomás Amat Guarinos, Oliviero Godi, Maha Kutay, Clarissa Matthews, Graham Modlen, Anne Save de Beaurecueil, Leena Ibrahim

TOTAL FLOOR AREA 120 m²

STRUCTURAL ENGINEER Ove Arup and Partners – Rob Devey, Shiguru Hikone, Colin Jackson, Darren Sri-Tharan, Jane Wernick

QUANTITY SURVEYOR Tillyard – Brett Butler

COMPUTER IMAGES Flexagon Studio – Thomas Quihano, Wassim Halabi

PRADO MUSEUM EXTENSION
Madrid, 1996

DESIGN TEAM Zaha Hadid with Tomás Amat Guarinos, Patrik Schumacher, Joaquin López, Ivan Pajares Sanchez, Anne Save de Beaurecueil, Markus Dochantschi, David Gomersall, Wassim Halabi, Paul Karakusevic, Simon Koumjian, Maha Kutay, Graham Modlen, Woody K.T. Yao, Simon Yu

SPANISH DESIGN TEAM Jesús Bermejo, Luis A. Gutiérrez, Juan Carlos Rico

CARDIFF BAY OPERA HOUSE
Cardiff, Wales, 1994–96
1900-seat Auditorium and Full Rehearsal Facilities, including Community Wing, Public Concourse and Restaurants

CLIENT Cardiff Bay Opera House Trust, The Rt Hon Lord Crickhowell – Chairman

DESIGN Zaha Hadid

PROJECT ARCHITECT Brian Ma Siy

DESIGN TEAM Patrik Schumacher, Ljiljana Blagojevic, Graham Modlen, Paul Brislin, Edgar Gonzalez, Paul Karakusevic, David Gomersall, Tomás Amat Guarinos, Wendy Ing, Paola Sanguinetti, Nunu Luan, Douglas Grieco, Woody K.T. Yao, Voon Yee-Wong, Anne Save de Beaurecueil, Simon Koumjian, Bijan Ganjei, Nicola Cousins

MODELS Ademir Volic, Michael Kennedy, James Wink

TOTAL FLOOR AREA 25,000 m²

PERCY THOMAS PARTNERSHIP Ian Peperell, Richard Roberts, Russell Baker, Richard Puckrin

PROJECT MANAGER Stanhope Properties – Peter Rogers

ACOUSTIC CONSULTANT Arup Acoustics – Richard Cowell, Nigel Cogger

THEATRE CONSULTANT Theatre Projects Consultants – David Staples, Alan Russell, Anne Minors

STRUCTURAL ENGINEER Ove Arup and Partners – Jane Wernick, David Glover, John Lovell

SERVICES CONSULTANT Ove Arup and Partners – Simon Hancock

QUANTITY SURVEYOR Gardiner & Theobald & Tillyard – Brett Butler, Peter Coxall

ARTS CONSULTANT AEA – Adrian Ellis, Jan Billington
BRIEF CONSULTANT Inter Consult Culture – Charlotte Nassim
CONSTRUCTION MANAGER Bovis Lehrer McGovern – Alan Lansdell

BOILERHOUSE EXTENSION, VICTORIA AND ALBERT MUSEUM
London, 1996
Exhibition Galleries, Lecture Theatre/Cinema, Orientation Centre, Restaurants, Administration, Education Facilities
CLIENT Victoria and Albert Museum
DESIGN TEAM Zaha Hadid with Patrik Schumacher, Brian Ma Siy, Graham Modlen, Ljiljana Blagojevic, Paul Karakusevic, David Gomersall, Woody K.T. Yao, Markus Dochantschi, Wassim Halabi, Ivan Pajares Sanchez, Maha Kutay, Simon Yu, Tomás Amat Guarinos, James Geiger, Tilman Schall, Alan Houston
TOTAL FLOOR AREA 10,000 m²
STRUCTURAL ENGINEER Ove Arup and Partners – Jane Wernick
COST CONSULTANT Davis Langdon Everest – Rob Smith
BUILDING SERVICES Ove Arup and Partners – Simon Hancock
CONSTRUCTION MANAGEMENT Ove Arup and Partners (PMS) – Peter Platt-Higgins

WISH MACHINE: WORLD INVENTION
Kunsthalle, Vienna, 1996
Exhibition Design for 'A History of Techno-Visions since the 18th Century'
CLIENT Kunsthalle Wien – Herbert Lachmeyer; curator, Brigitte Felderer
DESIGN TEAM Zaha Hadid with Patrik Schumacher and Simon Yu, Wassim Halabi, Markus Dochantschi, David Gomersall, Woody K.T. Yao, Paul Karakusevic
TOTAL FLOOR AREA 900 m²

PAPER ART
Leopold-Hoesch-Museum, Düren, Germany, 1996
Exhibition
DESIGN TEAM Zaha Hadid with Markus Dochantschi, Yousif Albustani, Shumon Basar, Matthias Sachau
INSTALLATION TEAM Markus Dochantschi, Helmut Lutsch

MASTER'S SECTION
Venice Biennale, Palazzo Grassi, Venice, 1996
Exhibition
DESIGN TEAM Zaha Hadid with Patrik Schumacher, Markus Dochantschi, Woody K.T. Yao, Wassim Halabi, Garin O'Aivazian, David Gomersall, Simon Yu, Yousif Albustani, Guiseppe Anzalone Gherardi

HABITABLE BRIDGE
London, 1996
Mixed-use Development (Offices, Flats, Bars/Cafés, Nightclubs, Shops, Galleries)
SPONSOR Thames Water
CLIENT The Secretary of State, The Rt Hon John Gummer and The Royal Academy

DESIGN TEAM Zaha Hadid with Patrik Schumacher, Ljiljana Blagojevic, Paul Karakusevic, Graham Modlen, Woody K.T. Yao, Markus Dochantschi, Tilman Schall, Colin Harris, Thilo Fuchs, Shumon Basar, Katrin Kalden, Anne-Marie Foster
MODELS Alan Houston, Michael Howe
COMPUTER DESIGN Wassim Halabi, Simon Yu, Garin O'Aivazian
TOTAL FLOOR AREA 40,000 m²
STRUCTURAL ENGINEER Ove Arup and Partners – Jane Wernick, Sophie Le Bourva
SERVICES CONSULTANT Ove Arup and Partners – Simon Hancock, Dorte Rich Jorgensen
TRANSPORTATION CONSULTANT Ove Arup and Partners – John Shaw
MANAGEMENT Ove Arup and Partners (PMS) – Harry Saradjian
COST CONSULTANT Davis Langdon and Everest – Rob Smith, Sam MacKenzie

LA FENICE
Venice, 1996
Painting
DESIGN TEAM Zaha Hadid with Graham Modlen, Maha Kutay and Simon Yu
COMPUTER DESIGN Wassim Halabi

PHILHARMONIC HALL
Luxembourg, 1997
CLIENT Ministry of Public Buildings, Luxembourg
ARCHITECTS Zaha Hadid with Patrik Schumacher
DESIGN TEAM Garin O'Aivazian, Markus Dochantschi, Woody K.T. Yao, Wassim Halabi, Jan Hubener, Anna Klingmann, Tilman Schall, Filipe Pereira, Shumon Basar, Mark Hemel, Yousif Albustani, Graham Modlen, Anuschka Kutz, David Gomersall
TOTAL FLOOR AREA 7,100 m²

LANDESGARTENSCHAU 1999
Weil am Rhein, Germany, 1997–
Exhibition Space, Café, Centre of Enviromental Research
CLIENT Landesgartenschau Weil am Rhein GmbH
ARCHITECT Zaha Hadid with Patrik Schumacher, Mayer Bährle
PROJECT ARCHITECT Markus Dochantschi
PROJECT TEAM Oliver Domeisen, Wassim Halabi, Garin O'Aivazian, Barbara Pfennigsdorf, James Lim
MODEL June Tamura, Jim Heverin, Jon Richards, Ademir Volic
TOTAL FLOOR AREA 800 m²

MUSEUM OF ISLAMIC ARTS
Doha, Qatar, 1997
CLIENT State of Qatar
ARCHITECTS Zaha Hadid with Patrik Schumacher and Woody K.T. Yao
DESIGN TEAM Shumon Basar, Graham Modlen, Markus Dochantschi, Anuschka Kutz, Garin O'Aivazian, Filipe Pereira, Ivan Pajares Sanchez, Wassim Halabi, Ali Mangera, Edgardo Torres, Julie Fisher, Andrew Schachman, Oliver Domeisen, Julie Richards, Irene Huttenrauch, Tia Lindgren
TOTAL FLOOR AREA 28,000 m²

HACKNEY EMPIRE
London, 1997
DESIGN TEAM Zaha Hadid, Markus Dochantschi, Graham Modlen, Anuschka Kutz, Oliver Domeisen, Irene Huttenrauch, Woody K.T. Yao, Patrik Schumacher, David Gomersall, Tia Lindgren

CAMPUS CENTRE
Illinois Institute of Technology, Chicago, 1998
ARCHITECTURAL DESIGN Zaha Hadid with Patrik Schumacher
DESIGN TEAM Yousif Albustani, Anuschka Kutz, Oliver Domeisen, Shumon Basar, Inken Witt, Jee-Eun Lee, Wassim Halabi, Ivan Pajares Sanchez, David Gomersall, Stephane Hof, Woody K.T. Yao, Markus Dochantschi, Marco Guarnieri, Ali Mangera, Jim Heverin, John Richards, Terence Koh, Simon Yu, James Lim, Tilman Schall
CHARTERED QUANTITY SURVEYORS Davis Langdon and Everest, Partner – Sam Mackenzie with Brian Irving
STRUCTURAL AND CIVIL ENGINEERING Ove Arup and Partners – Jane Wernick
BUILDING SERVICES Ove Arup and Partners – Simon Hancock
ACOUSTICS Arup Acoustics – Andrew Nicol
CONSTRUCTION MANAGEMENT Ove Arup and Partners – Peter Platt-Higgins
FIRE AND MEANS OF ESCAPE Ove Arup and Partners – Chris Barber,
INFORMATION TECHNOLOGY Ove Arup and Partners – Volker Buscher
URBAN CONTEXT REPORT Space Syntax Laboratory, UCL, London – Bill Hillier, Mark David Major

CONTEMPORARY ARTS CENTRE
Cincinnati, 1998–
ARCHITECTURAL DESIGN Zaha Hadid
COMPETITION TEAM Shumon Basar, Oliver Domeisen, Jee-Eun Lee, Terence Koh, Marco Guarinieri, Stephane Hof, Woody K.T. Yao, Wassim Halabi, Nan Atichapong
DESIGN DEVELOPMENT TEAM Michael Wolfson, Shumon Basar, Markus Dochantschi, Patrik Schumacher, Jee-Eun Lee, Oliver Domeisen
CHARTERED QUANTITY SURVEYOR Davis Langdon and Everest
STRUCTURAL AND CIVIL ENGINEERING Ove Arup and Partners
BUILDING SERVICES Ove Arup and Partners
ACOUSTICS Ove Arup and Partners
THEATRE CONSULTANT Ann Minors

PHOTOGRAPHY CREDITS

Unless otherwise stated, all photographs of models, paintings and line drawings have been taken by Edward Woodman.

Hélène Binet: 2, 60, 66–67, 110–14, 131
Richard Bryant/Arcaid: 30
Markus Dochantschi: 132–33
Herman van Doorn: 72–73
Christian Richter: 38–39
Paul Warchol: 56–59, 83

1992 Gallery Plan Venise, Paris; 'Vitra', Aedes Galerie und Architekturforum, Berlin; 'Dimensions Expanded and Explored', Rijksmuseum Kröller-Müller, Otterlo, The Netherlands; 'Madrid European Cultural Capital 1992', Madrid

1993 'I Am the Enunciator', Thread Waxing Gallery, New York; 'New World Images', Louisiana Museum of Modern Art, Denmark; 'Re-opening', Museum für Angewandte Kunst, Vienna

1994 Graduate School of Design, Harvard University; Architectural Association, London; 'An Opera House for Wales', National Museum of Wales, Cardiff, and the Independent Television Network Building, London

1995 Grand Central Station, New York; 'In Dialog: Zeichnungen zur Spittelau', Vienna; Galerie Grita Insam and Galerie Billie Strauss, Nabern, Germany; Fourth Istanbul Biennale; 'European Architecture 1984–94', Istanbul; Fondacio Mies Van Der Rohe, Barcelona; 'Project Pfaffenberg-Carnuntum Museum', Architektur Zentrum, Vienna

1996 'Zaha Hadid: Recent Projects 1990–95', Galerie Renate Kammer, Hamburg; 'Products of Desire 2', Royal Institute of British Architects, London; 'The Summer Exhibition 1996', Royal Academy of Arts, London; 'Tribute to Philip Johnson', Museum of Modern Art, New York; Venice Architecture Biennale

1997 'Cities of the Future: Towards New Urban Living', travelling exhibition to Hong Kong, South Korea, China, Singapore, Philippines, Taiwan and Japan; 'GA International '97', GA Gallery, Tokyo; 'Creating Utopia', Davies Memorial Gallery, Newtown, Wales; 'Architektur Sommer', Galerie Renate Kammer, Hamburg

1998 Retrospective, Museum of Modern Art, San Francisco; 'At the End of the Century: One Hundred Years of Architecture', The Museum of Contemporary Art, Tokyo; Galerie Grita Insam, Vienna; The Contemporary Art Centre, Cincinnati

PUBLICATIONS

1984 *A III Times* [school magazine] (Mar); *AA Files* (May, no. 6); *L'Architecture d'aujourd'hui* (Jun, no. 233); *Architektur Visionen* (Aug); *Ausstellung* (Sep); *Blueprint* (Dec–Jan); *Casa* (Spring); *Domus* (May, no. 650); *Hermes* (Dec); *Progressive Architecture* (Oct); *Wohen Tabk* (Aug)

1985 *The Architects' Journal* (Aug, no. 34–35); *L'Architecture d'aujourd'hui* (Dec); *Architecture and Urbanism* (Dec, no. 183); *Architectures* (Winter, no. 1); *Contemporary Landscape* (9 Oct); *Domus* (Sep, no. 643); *Exhibition Paris Biennale Catalogue* (Apr); *The Face*, (May); *GA Document* (Sep, no. 13); *Les Immateriaux*, (Mar); *Interni* (Aug, no. 352); *Plan*, (Apr); *La Riconstruzione della Città* (Electra Editrice); *S.D.* (May); *Space Design*, (May); *XVII Triennale di Milano* (Feb)

1986 *AA Files* (Summer, no. 12); *Architectural Review* (Jan); *Colloquim Architecture Modernism En De Stadt* (Oct); *GA Architect* [monograph] (no. 5); *Modern Redux* (4 Mar–19 Apr)

1987 *AA Files* (Summer, no. 15); *Archis* (Jun); *The Architects' Journal* (Aug, no. 33); *Architectural Record* (Jun); *Architectural Review* (Apr); *L'Architecture d'aujourd'hui* (Sep, no. 252); *Architecture and Urbanism* (Sep, no. 204); *Bauwelt* (23 Oct); *Blueprint* (Nov, no. 42); *Casa Vogue* (Nov, no. 190); *Jahrbuch für Architektur* (Deutsches Architektur Museum); *Metropolis* (Jul–Aug); *Stern* (Sep)

1988 *Ambiente* (Feb); *Arch+* (Nov–Dec, nos 96/97); *Architectural Design* (vol. 58, nos 3/4); *Architecture Intérieure Créé* (Oct–Nov, no. 1307); *Architectural Record* (mid-Sep); *Archithese* (Jan–Feb); *Avenue* (Nov, no. 4); *Basler* (19 Mar, no. 12); *Baumeister* (May); *Blitz* (Sep, no. 69); *Blueprint* (Jul–Aug, no. 49); *Chicago Tribune* (25 Sep); *Eastern Review* (Sep); *Elle* (Apr, no. 8); *Emois* (Mar, no. 9); *Frankfurter Allgemeine* (Jul); *Galleria Di Architettura* (Sep–Oct, no. 8); *The Guardian* (8 Apr); *Harpers and Queen* (Jan); *House and Garden* (Sep, no. 9); *ID: Magazine of International Design* (Nov–Dec); *The Independent* (29 Jun); *Interni* (Sep, no. 383); *Interni* (Dec, no. 386); *Metropolitan Home* (Apr, no. 4); *Metropolitan Home* (Aug, no. 8); *Metropolitan Home* (Dec, no. 12); *Modo* (Jun–Jul, no. 107); *Neue Züricher Zeitung* (Jul); *The New York Times Magazine* (12 Jul); *Schöner Wohnen* (12 Dec); *The Sunday Times Magazine* [house style supplement]

(Autumn); *Taxi* (Jun–Jul, no. 6–7); *Vogue* (Sep); *Westside* (Feb)

1989 *AA Files* (Spring, no. 17); *Archithese* (Jan–Feb); *Architektur und Wohnen* (Jul–Aug); *Arkitektens Forlag* (Feb, no. 2–3); *Arquitectura* (Aug); *Artforum* (Summer, no. 10); *Artikekt Foretaget*, (no. 2); *Axis* (Winter); *Blueprint* (Jan); *Building Design* (4 Aug); *Building Design* (8 Dec); *Designers' Journal* (Feb, no. 44); *Imara Architectural Quarterly* (Feb); *Interior Design* (no. 17); *Modo* (Sep, no. 116); *Oz* (vol. 9); *Savvy Woman* (Mar); *Telescope* (Autumn); *Vis à Vis* (Apr, vol. 3, no. 4)

1990 *Architectural Design* (no. 87); *Bo Bedre* (May); *Brutus* (1 Jan); *Building Design* (9 Feb); *Building Design* (11 May); *Continental* (May); *Corriere della Sera* (21 Jul, no. 29); *Daidalos* (Sep, no. 37); *Düsseldorfer Illustrierte* (Feb, no. 2); *Fusion Planning* (Jul); *The Guardian* (18 Feb); *Ha'Aretz* (Mar); *House and Garden* (Feb, no. 2); *The Japan Architect* (no. 5); *The Japan Architect* (no. 9); *Kukan* (Sep, no. 9); *Kunchika* (Mar, no. 521); *Le Moniteur Architecture* (Feb, no. 8); *S.D.* (Mar); *Shotenkenchiku* (Sep, no. 9); *Space Design* (Mar, no. 306); *Space Design* (May, no. 308); *37 Contemporary Architects*, (Fukutake Books); *Suddeutsche Zeitung* (Jul); *Vogue* (Sep); *What a Wonderful World* (Sep); *Wiener* (5 May); *World Architecture*, (vol. 1, no. 4)

1991 *AA Osaka Follies* [catalogue]; *Architectural Journal* (30 Jan); *Architectural Review* (Nov, no. 1137); *Arquitectura Viva* (Jul–Aug, no. 19); *Architecture Today* (15 Feb); *Baumeister* (Jan); *Bauwelt* (11 Jan); *Building Design* (1 Mar); *El Croquis* [monograph] (Dec, no. 52); *Diseño Interior* (Sep, no. 7); *Domus* (Jul–Aug, no. 729); *Elle Decoration* (Summer, no. 12); *House and Garden* (Apr, no. 4); *Progressive Architecture* (Feb); *Urbanism and Industrial Culture, International Workshop* (Birkhäuser); *Vogue* (Jun, vol. 155, no. 2316)

1992 *AIT* (Jun, no. 6192); *au (Arquitectura e Urbanismo)* (Dec 91–Jan 92, no. 39); *Architectural Design* (vol. 62, nos 3–4); *Architectural Design: Free Space Architecture* (Academy Editions); *Deutsche Bauzeitung* (Jan); *Harper's Bazaar* (Oct); *Newsline* (Mar–Apr); *Progressive Architecture* (Oct)

1993 *AIT* (Jun); *Abitare* (Sep); *Archis* (Oct); *Architectural Review* (Jun, vol. CXIII, no. 1156); *Architecture* (Sep, vol. 82, no. 9); *L'Architecture d'aujourd'hui* (Sep, no. 288); *Architecture & Technique* (Sep); *Architecture Today* (Oct, no. 42); *Architecture & Urbanism* (Feb); *Architecture & Urbanism* (Oct); *Architektur & Wohnen* (Aug–Sep); *ART* (Jun); *Art in America* (May, vol. 81, no.

5); *Basler Magazin* (15 May); *Baumeister* (Sep); *Bauwelt* (4 Jun, no. 2); *Blick* (19 May); *Blueprint* (Jun); *Building Design* (14 May); *Bühne* (May); *Bündner Zeitung* (15 May); *Contemporary European Architects*, (vol. 2, Taschen); *De Architect* (Dec); *Der Spiegel* (17 May, no. 20); *Die Zeit* (21 May); *Domus* (Sep); *Frankfurter Allgemeine Zeitung* (14 May); *Global Architecture* (no. 37); *Graphis* (Sep–Oct, vol. 49, no. 287); *The Guardian* (17 May); *Jahresbroschüre 93–94: Meisterklasse für Experimentelle Visuelle Gestaltung*; *Leonardo* (Sep); *Louisiana Revy* (Feb, no. 2); *Neue Züricher Zeitung* (2 Jun); *The New York Times Magazine* (16 May); *Le Nouveau Quotidien* (15 May); *The Observer* (23 May); *Progressive Architecture* (Aug); *Stadt Bauwelt* (24 Sep, no. 119); *Stern* (27 May, no. 22); *The Structurist* (nos 33–34); *Studio, The Berlage Cahiers 3: The New Private Realm* (no. 010); *Süddeutsche Zeitung* (18 May); *Tages-Anzeiger* (15 May); *Vogue* (Aug)

1994 *AA Files* (no. 27); *AIT* (Jan–Feb); *AXIS* (Autumn, vol. 53); *Arch+* (Dec); *Archetype* (Oct); *Archis* (Dec); *The Architects' Journal* (22 Sep, no. 11); *The Architects' Journal* (6 Oct, no. 13); *The Architects' Journal* (27 Oct, no. 16); *Architecture* (Oct); *Architecture* (Nov); *Architecture Today* (Oct, no. 52); *d'Architectures* (Jan–Feb, no. 42); *Architektur* (Oct); *Architektur & Technik* (Feb); *Architektura & Biznes* (no. 9); *Arena* (Dec 94–Jan 95, no. 49); *Arquitectura & Diseño* (26 Jan); *Arquitectura Viva* (May–Jun, no. 36); *Arquitectura Viva* (Nov, no. 39); *Blueprint* (Autumn, no. 11); *Building Design* (16 Sep, no. 1190); *Construction Moderne* (no. 79); *Design Quarterly* (Summer, no.161); *Deutsche Bauzeitschrift* (Feb); *Deutsche Bauzeitschrift* (Nov); *Diseño Interior* (Nov, no. 40); *Du* (Nov–Dec, no. 11); *FX* (Nov, no. 17); *Focus* (8 Aug, no. 32); *Global Architecture* (no. 41); *Hia Magazine* (Jul); *L'Industria delle Constructioni* (Aug); *Industrial Workshop Vitra/Weil am Rhein* (Birkhäuser); *Nordic Building and Construction* (no. 3); *Das Österreichische Fachmagazin Architektur* (Nov); *Progressive Architecture* (Dec); *Tate, the Art Magazine* (Spring, no. 2); *Vogue* (Jan, no. 2346)

1995 *Anons* (Aug, nos 53–54); *L'Arca* (Mar, no. 91); *de Architect* (Mar); *The Architects' Journal* (12 Jan, no. 2); *The Architects' Journal* (26 Jan, no. 4); *The Architects' Journal* (27 Apr, no. 17); *Architectural Digest* (Oct, no. 10); *Architecture and Urbanism* (Aug, no. 299); *L'Architecture d'aujourd'hui* (Apr, no. 298); *Architektur Aktuell* (Jan–Feb, nos 175–76); *Architektur Aktuell* (May, no. 179); *Arquitectura*

(Aug–Sep, no. 13); *Art Forum International* (Feb); *Art in America* (Jul, no. 7); *Baumeister* (Mar); *Bauwelt* (11 Aug, nos 29–30); *Bodenreform 3 (Original Floor Design Created by Artists and Architects)* (Koch); *Building Design* (28 Apr, no. 1218); *Building Design* (10 Nov, no. 1242); *Cambridge Architecture Journal* (no. 7); *El Croquis* [monograph] (Sep); *Deutsche Bauzeitung* (Jan); *Harpers and Queen* (May); *Journal of Architecture and Building Science* (Nov, no. 1380); *Korean Architects* (May, no. 129); *Leonardo* (May); *Mediagramm* (Jan, no. 18); *New York* (6 Mar, no. 10); *Oculus* (Mar, vol. 57, no. 7); *Progressive Architecture* (Feb); *South Wales Echo* (18 Apr); *The Spectator* (18 Mar, no. 8697); *Vogue* (Oct, no. 761); *Werk, Bauen and Wohnen* (May); *Wired* (Sep)

1996 *Al Handasah* (Nov, no. 106); *The Architects' Journal* (19 Sep, no. 10); *Architectural Digest* (Jan); *Architectural Profile*; *Architektur Aktuell*; *Architektur+Wettbewerbe* (Dec, no. 168); *Blueprint* [supplement] (Oct); *Building* (Jan, no. 7924); *Building Design* (Jan, no. 1249); *Building Design* (Mar, no. 1256); *The Guardian* (3 Aug); *Harper's Bazaar* (Oct, no. 3419); *Häuser* (May); *The J. Paul Getty Trust Bulletin* [Los Angeles]; *South* (Nov); *Time* (Oct)

1997 *AJ AA 150 Special Issue* (Jul); *Abitare* (May, no. 362); *The Architects' Journal* (9 Jan); *The Architects' Journal* (24 Apr); *The Architects' Journal* (26 Jun); *The Architects' Journal* (17 Jul); *The Architects' Journal,* (16 Oct); *Architecture* (Jun, no. 6); *Architecture Today* (Jun); *Architektur* (Jun); *Architektur & Wohnen Prominenz auf Abwegen* (Hamburg); *Art 4d* (Mar, no. 25); *Art in America* (Jul); *Bauwelt* (12 Dec, no. 47); *Building Design* (Jul); *Building Design* (21 Nov); *Design for Living* (17 May); *Design Report* (May); *Deutsche Bauzeitschrift* (Feb); *Dialogue Magazine* (Apr); *Drawing on Diversity: Women Architecture & Practice* (London); *Forum* (May–Jun, no. 176); *FX: Design in Business & Society*; *The International Design Yearbook* (Laurence King); *Restaurants in New York, USA and Japan* (New York and Milan); *Ein Haus, Ein Aufuhr* (May); *Interiors* (Summer); *Los Angeles Times* (30 Dec); *Nikkei Architecture* (20 Oct, no. 594); *Rivista tecnica l'architettura di Vitra* (Lugano); *Building Design* (May); *Wall Street Journal* (9 Apr)

1998 *AIT* (Apr); *AU* (Jul, no. 334); *Building Design* (12 Feb); *The Architects' Journal* (12 Feb); *The Architectural Review* (Mar); *Diseño Interior* (Jan); *The New York Times* (13 Mar); *The New York Times* (25 Mar); *Al Hayat* (12 Apr); *Building Design* (Mar)

VITA

Zaha Hadid studied architecture at the Architectural Association (AA) from 1972 and was awarded the Diploma Prize in 1977. After graduation she was a partner in the Office for Metropolitan Architecture (OMA) with Rem Koolhaas and Elia Zenghelis and taught at the AA; she later led her own studio there until 1987. Hadid's academic engagements continue to the present, with visiting professorships, master classes and lectures at institutions around the world. In 1994, she held the Kenzo Tange Chair at the Graduate School of Design, Harvard University, Cambridge, Massachusetts); she was awarded the 1997 Sullivan Chair at the University of Chicago School of Architecture. Currently, Hadid holds a guest professorship at the Hochschule für Bildende Künste, Hamburg, and teaches a Masters Studio at Columbia University, New York.

Hadid has tested the boundaries of architectural design in a series of research-based competitions. Her work was awarded wide international recognition in 1983 with a winning entry for The Peak, Hong Kong. This was followed by first-place awards for competitions for a mixed-used development on Kurfürstendamm in Berlin (1986) and for the Cardiff Bay Opera House (1994) in Wales. In parallel to her theoretical and academic work, Hadid established her own practice in 1979 with the design for an apartment in Eaton Place, London (1982), for which she won the Architectural Design Gold Medal. In 1990, Hadid completed a Music Video Pavilion in Groningen, The Netherlands. She created the installation for the *Great Utopia* exhibition at the Solomon R. Guggenheim Museum, New York (1992), which was followed by the Pavilion for *Blueprint Magazine* (1995), built for the Interbuild exhibition in Birmingham. Hadid's first major built project was a fire station for the Vitra furniture company, which opened in 1993 to great public and critical acclaim. That year, Hadid also completed one of the last housing projects for the IBA–Block 2 in Berlin.

Hadid's paintings and drawings have always been an important medium for the exploration of her design. Beginning with a large retrospective at the AA (1983), her work has been included in major exhibitions around the world. It is also in the permanent collections of the Museum of Modern Art (New York), the Deutsches Architektur Museum (Frankfurt), the Museum of Modern Art (San Francisco), and the Getty Trust (Los Angeles).

Competition honours include short-listed finalist for the Victoria and Albert Museum's new Boilerhouse Gallery and the Luxembourg Concert Hall (fourth prize). Hadid's office also won a joint first prize for the Thames Water–Royal Academy Habitable Bridge international architectural competition. In 1998, she was a finalist for a competition to build a new student campus centre at the Illinois Institute of Technology, Chicago. Most recently, her office has been selected to design a new contemporary arts centre in downtown Cincinnati, which will be the first museum in the United States designed by a woman.